T0115207

SHOW ME THE MONEY

LEADERSHIP: FROM BLUE-COLLAR TO WHITE-COLLAR THINKING

Reginald Ramsey, PhD, MBA, CISA

authorHOUSE®

AuthorHouse™
1663 Liberty Drive
Bloomington, IN 47403
www.authorhouse.com
Phone: 833-262-8899

Published by AuthorHouse 04/27/2021

ISBN: 978-1-6655-2443-8 (sc)
ISBN: 978-1-6655-2448-3 (e)

Library of Congress Control Number: 2021908788

Print information available on the last page.

Any people depicted in stock imagery provided by Getty Images are models, and such images are being used for illustrative purposes only.
Certain stock imagery © Getty Images.

This book is printed on acid-free paper.

Disclaimer

This book is not intended for everyone! If you are not interested in learning how to navigate or change from blue-collar to white-collar thinking, this book is not for you. Let me reiterate: if you are interested in learning how to change or transition from a blue-collar thought process to a white-collar thinking process, this book is for you! In my upcoming books, I will target other topics. However, in this book, it is solely regarding the skills, attributes, and talents that it takes to transition or change from blue-collar to white-collar thinking. You will find stories from others who shared their experience making this transition.

This book is dedicated to my beautiful and loving wife, Lora A. Ramsey. Thank you for pushing and encouraging me to get this book written. This book is also dedicated to my mom and dad, Florence and Minor C. Ramsey Jr.; my granddaughter, Azaria La'nay Ramsey—she will be a great lady; my cousin Randy Rene Tillis; my auntie Alice Tillis; my grandparents, Daniel "Buddy" Hammond Sr., Ruth Hammond, and Lottie P. and Minor Ramsey Sr.; and, finally, my tennis coach, Mr. George "Tuffy" Clark. He helped me to grow beyond the game of tennis.

It is not the critic who counts; not the man who points out how the strong man stumbles, or where the doer of deeds could have done them better. The credit belongs to the man who is actually in the arena, whose face is marred by dust and sweat and blood; who strives valiantly; who errs, who comes short again and again, because there is no effort without error and shortcoming; but who does actually strive to do the deeds; who knows great enthusiasm, the great devotions; who spends himself in a worthy cause; who at the best knows in the end the triumph of high achievement, and who at the worst, if he fails, at least fails while daring greatly, so that his place shall never be with those cold and timid souls who neither know victory nor defeat.
—Theodore Roosevelt

As a Man thinketh so is he.
—Proverbs 23:7

Marketing appeal or target audience:

1) Military personnel
2) Foreign nationals
3) Colleges
4) Universities
5) HBCUs
6) High schools
7) Trade schools
8) Global companies
9) Government agencies
10) Wall Street
11) Ivy League colleges/universities
12) Among others.

CONTENTS

PREFACE

What does success in the marketplace look like to you? Is your definition of *success* measured in terms of money, fame, fortune, good health, or all of the above? Everyone has a unique perspective on what success looks like. *Success* can be defined very differently by different people.

In this book, *success* is defined as one pursuing one's life purpose and passion. Success is more than the pursuit of money, fame, and fortune. Success, as it relates to this book, refers to one establishing and working to achieve one's individual life goals. These goals may come in different forms for each individual. They may come in one's career, family, health, or financial security. Success is a personal choice. Your success is a personal decision that only you can make. This book will highlight and illustrate some of the skills, attributes, and talents that it takes to transition or change from blue-collar to white-collar thinking. It is intended for this specific audience.

The author understands and appreciates that some individuals do not want to change from blue-collar to white-collar thinking. As such, this book is not intended for them. The author will share the mistakes he made and the lessons he learned while he figured out how to navigate from blue- to white-collar thinking. It was not an easy journey. He was constantly questioning why he had to change. This was a major internal battle and struggle. He wanted to "keep it real" in his culture, but he also wanted to learn how to successfully navigate from blue- to white-collar thinking as well. This was a difficult choice.

Why was this distinction between blue- and white-collar thinking so important to him? He had worked very hard in grade school, middle school, junior high, senior high, and college. He graduated from college with a bachelor of science in electronic engineering technology.

After graduation, the author received several job offers, including one with a major Fortune 500 company. He received an above average salary and bonuses in 1987. He was only twenty-one years old. He thought he would work hard and get rewarded with promotions and other perks; however, this was not the case. To be perfectly honest, the author did not understand the white-collar working environment. He relied on the teachings of his parents and grandparents. They told him to work hard, and people would see his hard work and reward it with promotions and bonuses, but this concept of "working hard" did not yield any results for nearly eight years of the author's career.

As such, he struggled to navigate the white-collar corporate terrain. This was very frustrating. After approximately eight years, the author did a self-check and self-analysis to see where he had gone wrong. It appeared that he was being "played" by the white-collar corporate world. He wanted to learn how to play the white-collar corporate game.

He learned the importance of effective mentoring. He learned how each mentor and sponsor can help or hurt career advancement. Not all mentors and sponsors are alike. It is a smart idea to select a mentor or sponsor very wisely and prudently. In addition, the relationship between the mentor and mentee must be a two-way street. Both parties must get something out of the relationship in order for it to grow and thrive. In short, it should be a reciprocal relationship.

The primary role of the mentor or coach is to help the mentee to learn the inner workings of the company or organization. This is vitally important to the mentee's growth and development.

As such, he pursued successful individuals, both White and Black, female and male. The author wanted to learn from others and was willing to open up and ask for help. It was not easy to ask for help, but he was determined to change and thrive in the white-collar corporate game. The author was willing to put his pride aside to grow and learn. He pursued successful individuals with a passion and established mentor and mentee relationships. He joined various organizations, such as Toastmasters

International. He took several courses on personal development—namely, crucial conversations. The author enrolled in an MBA program. He was very serious about changing his career trajectory and wanted to be in a position to help others as well.

In addition, the author wanted to become more aware of the unwritten rules and norms of the white-collar organizational environment. To this end, he pursued mentors, coaches, and other means to learn how to play and understand the white-collar corporate game.

Unfortunately, the author learned too many lessons by trial and error. He would like to show readers how to avoid the aggravation and sleepless nights by helping them learn what he did not know in his twenties, thirties, and forties. Keep in mind that the author did not know many of these social norms.

He was a product of a blue-collar working-class family and was not exposed to the white-collar corporate environment as a child. As such, he had to learn while he was on the job. This is not the preferred method for learning about the game of white-collar corporate politics. But he did not consider himself to be a victim. Instead, he is a student of the white-collar working environment.

The information provided in this book will help readers to save time, money, and effort in making the change from blue-collar to white-collar thinking. The author looks forward to hearing from readers and would especially like to receive positive and constructive feedback on the content of this book.

Please keep an open mind. Be willing to consider the content of this book. It is acceptable to disagree with the author's insights, but please be willing to change and grow. Happy reading!

Please review the thirty-eight responses to the author's questionnaire from successful and not-so-successful individuals. Readers can decide whether an individual is successful. What are some of the patterns? Use these patterns to identify the components of the art of success.

CHAPTER 1

INTRODUCTION

This book is dedicated and targeted to the numerous military veterans who are making the transition from military to civilian life. Many of the military veterans went into the armed forces right out of high school. As such, they are not prepared for or experienced with the civilian white-collar environment. This book will help them to understand some of the means, methods, tools and ways that may assist them in their quest to succeed in a white-collar working environment.

Some of the material from this book comes from the author's PhD dissertation, *Correlative Study of Emotional Intelligence and the Career Intentions of First-Year School of Business Students*. As such, in some cases throughout this book, it may appear and sound somewhat technical. However, my advice is for you to use the material that is contained in this book as a guide or tool. The information that applies to you and your situation, please use it. However, the information that does not apply to you or your current situation, please disregard.

To start this book, I surveyed several individuals ranging from management to non-management. In addition, I surveyed veterans and non-veterans. This book will show how mentoring and coaching with a high degree of emotional intelligence can help one with the transition from blue collar to white-collar thinking.

Survey

The following is the blank questionnaire. This questionnaire includes thirty-three questions.

Blue- to White-Collar Thinking Interview (33 questions)

Name: _____

Response Date: _____

1) What is your official job title?
2) How long have you been in your current role?
3) What attributes or skills helped you to reach your current career level?
4) What does your typical day entail? Please elaborate as much as possible.
5) How many hours do you work per week?
6) What advice would you give to someone who wants to be in your position someday?
7) What has been the role of mentors or coaches in your career advancement?
8) How many mentors do you have or have you had over your career?
9) How often do you speak or communicate with your mentor?
10) How do you balance your work and life?
11) How often do you set goals?
12) What type of goals do you set?
13) How long have you been working in the marketplace?
14) What was your first job?
15) What valuable lessons have you learned over your career?
16) What type of spiritual life do you have?
17) Do you attend or engage in any religious activities?
18) What role has emotional intelligence played in your career progression?
19) What are some unwritten rules or norms you learned from being in a white-collar environment?
20) Did your parents or grandparents work in a white-collar setting?
21) Did your parents or grandparents teach you how to navigate a white-collar working environment?

22) What did your parents or grandparents teach you about working in a white-collar environment?

23) How did you learn about these unwritten rules and norms (observation, mentors, mistakes)?

24) Currently, how many individuals do you mentor?

25) How often do you listen or read about successful individuals?

26) What role has self-talk played in your career success?

27) How do you motivate yourself each day?

28) What are some of your hobbies?

29) Do you believe in the Performance, Image, Exposure (PIE) model for career success introduced in Harvey Coleman (2010) book?

30) How often do you exercise?

31) How much time do you take off each year to recharge your batteries?

32) May I use your name in the book? (keep confidential)

33) Whom would you recommend that I interview for this book?

Blue- to White-Collar Thinking Interview (33 Questions)

Name:____Male/Asian/Professional_____

Response Date: __9/21/2017_____

1) What is your official job title? Senior data manager
2) How long have you been in your current role? Ten years
3) What attributes or skills helped you to reach your current career level? Education, IT, listening to his heart over his fears
4) What does your typical day entail? Please elaborate as much as possible. Emails, phone calls, programming, presentations
5) How many hours do you work per week? Thirty-five to forty hours per week
6) What advice would you give to someone who wants to be in your position someday? "Network or not work," learn more than the basics.
7) What has been the role of mentors or coaches in your career advancement? Showed him the right path.
8) How many mentors do you have or have you had over your career? Four to five mentors
9) How often do you speak or communicate with your mentor? Not often now; was on a weekly basis.
10) How do you balance your work and life? "Me" time, find your "me" time; meditation.
11) How often do you set goals? Not often
12) What type of goals do you set? NA
13) How long have you been working in the marketplace? Twelve years
14) What was your first job? IT technology
15) What valuable lessons have you learned over your career? Connection, friends, being "present" and compassionate about others; check on your coworkers.
16) What type of spiritual life do you have? Learning to connect with his soul; listen to tapes (South Indian)

17) Do you attend or engage in any religious activities? Yes

18) What role has emotional intelligence played in your career progression? Big role; "don't be a victim," stay above the line.

19) What are some unwritten rules or norms that you learned from being in a white-collar environment? What is in your mind is not always true; manage your thoughts.

20) Did your parents or grandparents work in a white-collar setting? Yes or No? Father did; Mother did not.

21) Did your parents or grandparents teach you how to navigate a white-collar working environment? Work hard; he has the responsibility of their name.

22) What did your parents or grandparents teach you about working in a white-collar environment? Hard work; remember the story of the turtle and the rabbit.

23) How did you learn about these unwritten rules and norms (observation, mentors, mistakes)? Observation

24) Currently, how many individuals do you mentor? Three to four people

25) How often do you listen or read about successful individuals? Not often; used to be five to ten times per month

26) What role has self-talk played in your career success? Tell himself to get in front of 10,000 people.

27) How do you motivate yourself each day? Networking, true person, provide for his family and neighbors' kids

28) What are some of your hobbies? Cricket, volleyball, soccer

29) Do you believe in the PIE model for career success? Didn't work for him.

30) How often do you exercise? Three to four times per week

31) How much time do you take off each year to recharge your batteries? None

32) May I use your name in the book? (keep confidential)

33) Whom would you recommend that I interview for this book?

Blue- to White-Collar Thinking Interview (33 questions)
Send to Reginald Ramsey, PhD, MBA @ HRTC1906@gmail.com
Name:_____Black/Male/Executive_____
Response Date: __9/15/2017_____

1) What is your official job title? Executive sales professional
2) How long have you been in your current role? Eight years
3) What attributes or skills helped you to reach your current career level? Learning agility, effective communications
4) What does your typical day entail? Please, elaborate as much as possible. Sales, something different every day, working with customers, product fit
5) How many hours do you work per week? Thirty hours per week
6) What advice would you give to someone who wants to be in your position someday? Focus on the customer, convey to the customers, common sense.
7) What has been the role of mentors or coaches in your career advancement? Minimal, could have done better.
8) How many mentors do you have or have you had over your career? Minimal, few
9) How often do you speak or communicate with your mentor/s? Variable, monthly
10) How do you balance your work and life? Learned over time to know what is the most important, goal setting
11) How often do you set goals? Quarterly
12) What type of goals do you set? Yearly? Monthly? Self-development, retirement planning
13) How long have you been working in the market space? Twenty-seven years
14) What was your first job? Retail pharmacy
15) What valuable lessons have you learned over your career? Who you know is important.

16) What type of spiritual life do you have? Strong spiritual life

17) Do you attend or engage in any religious activities? Yes

18) What role has emotional intelligence played in your career progression? Critical, have a keen awareness

19) What are some unwritten rules or norms that you learned from being in a white-collar environment? Monitor and evaluate how you step up and adjust as needed.

20) Did your parents or grandparents work in a white-collar setting? Yes or No? Mom did.

21) Did your parents or grandparents teach you how to navigate a white-collar working environment? No

22) What did your parents or grandparents teach you about working in a white-collar environment? Put in your best effort.

23) How did you learn about these unwritten rules and norms (observation, mentors, mistakes)? No response

24) Currently, how many individuals do you mentor? Numerous

25) How often do you listen or read about successful individuals? Not that often

26) What role has self-talk played in your career success? Put your best foot forward.

27) How do you motivate yourself each day? Provide for family.

28) What are some of your hobbies? Golf, travel, community work

29) Do you believe in the PIE model for career success? Yes, would give more percentage to performance.

30) How often do you exercise? Not often enough

31) How much time do you take off each year to recharge your batteries? Six weeks per year

32) May I use your name in the book? (keep confidential) NA

33) Whom would you recommend that I interview for this book? NA

Blue- to White-Collar Thinking Interview (33 questions)
Send to Reginald Ramsey, PhD, MBA @ HRTC1906@gmail.com
Name:___Black/Male/Professional_____
Response Date: __9/26/2017_____

1) What is your official job title? Admission representative
2) How long have you been in your current role? One month
3) What attributes or skills helped you to reach your current career level? Effective communication, professionalism
4) What does your typical day entail? Please, elaborate as much as possible. Contact people, getting people interested in education/career development
5) How many hours do you work per week? Forty hours per week
6) What advice would you give to someone who wants to be in your position someday? Talk to a lot of people at their level, learn as much as you can, learn about people.
7) What has been the role of mentors or coaches in your career advancement? To be it, you have to see it; not all mentors know what they are talking about.
8) How many mentors do you have or have you had over your career? About ten
9) How often do you speak or communicate with your mentor/s? Regular basis, often
10) How do you balance your work and life? Understand what is most important, spend time with what is important
11) How often do you set goals? Not often enough
12) What type of goals do you set? Yearly? Monthly? Et cetera? NA
13) How long have you been working in the market space? Forty years
14) What was your first job? Indiana Bell
15) What valuable lessons have you learned over your career? Be true to yourself; find what you do, do it well.

16) What type of spiritual life do you have? It is the main part of what he does; everything is guided by his faith.

17) Do you attend or engage in any religious activities? Yes

18) What role has emotional intelligence played in your career progression? Very important part of his life; helps with his relationships; networking

19) What are some unwritten rules or norms that you learned from being in a white-collar environment? Dress code is important, important to observe; watch your facial hair in the workplace.

20) Did your parents or grandparents work in a white-collar setting? Yes or No? Mom worked in the office.

21) Did your parents or grandparents teach you how to navigate a white-collar working environment? Learned from his mother; don't take off work; come to work even if you are sick.

22) What did your parents or grandparents teach you about working in a white-collar environment? Same as 21

23) How did you learn about these unwritten rules and norms (observation, mentors, mistakes)? Mother

24) Currently, how many individuals do you mentor? Zero officially; however, he talks to schools when he is available.

25) How often do you listen or read about successful individuals? Quite often

26) What role has self-talk played in your career success? Very important; be your own best cheerleader.

27) How do you motivate yourself each day? It becomes normal and natural

28) What are some of your hobbies? Golf, reading, music, motorcycle

29) Do you believe in the PIE model for career success? Yes. He agreed with the model.

30) How often do you exercise? Not enough

31) How much time do you take off each year to recharge your batteries? Takes regular and consistent vacations
32) May I use your name in the book? (keep confidential) NA
33) Whom would you recommend that I interview for this book? NA

Blue- to White-Collar Thinking Interview (33 Questions)

Send to Reginald Ramsey, PhD, MBA @ HRTC1906@gmail.com

Name:_____Black/Male/Executive_____

Response Date: __10/31/2017_____

1) What is your official job title? Senior director

2) How long have you been in your current role? Four years

3) What attributes or skills helped you to reach your current career level? Critical thinking, business acumen, client relationship, project management

4) What does your typical day entail? Please, elaborate as much as possible. On the road 70 percent of the time, strategy

5) How many hours do you work per week? Sixty to sixty-five hours per week

6) What advice would you give to someone who wants to be in your position someday? Balance is the key; he chose career over relationships.

7) What has been the role of mentors or coaches in your career advancement? Critical; helped with feedback; sounding board

8) How many mentors do you have or have you had over your career? Currently three; had over thirty mentors

9) How often do you speak or communicate with your mentor/s? Monthly

10) How do you balance your work and life? Still learning

11) How often do you set goals? Annually

12) What type of goals do you set? Yearly? Monthly? Et cetera? Financial projections

13) How long have you been working in the market space? Thirty-seven years

14) What was your first job? Teacher, high school biology

15) What valuable lessons have you learned over your career? Don't forget the people you work with … all of them are jaded.

16) What type of spiritual life do you have? Christian

17) Do you attend or engage in any religious activities? Yes

18) What role has emotional intelligence played in your career progression? Very good factor; helps to read individuals, who to be cautious with; helps to play and survive in the corporate game.

19) What are some unwritten rules or norms that you learned from being in a white-collar environment? Accept that you are Black; self-awareness is key; manage yourself.

20) Did your parents or grandparents work in a white-collar setting? Yes or No? No

21) Did your parents or grandparents teach you how to navigate a white-collar working environment? No

22) What did your parents or grandparents teach you about working in a white-collar environment? NA

23) How did you learn about these unwritten rules and norms (observation, mentors, mistakes)? All of the above

24) Currently, how many individuals do you mentor? Four directly, ten to fifteen indirectly

25) How often do you listen or read about successful individuals? Daily

26) What role has self-talk played in your career success? NA

27) How do you motivate yourself each day? Love what he does.

28) What are some of your hobbies? Theater, movies, plays, reading

29) Do you believe in the PIE model for career success? No

30) How often do you exercise? Three times per week

31) How much time do you take off each year to recharge your batteries? Three to four weeks per year

32) May I use your name in the book? (keep confidential) NA

33) Whom would you recommend that I interview for this book? NA

Blue- to White-Collar Thinking Interview (33 questions)
Send to Reginald Ramsey, PhD, MBA @ HRTC1906@gmail.com
Name:_____Black/Female/Professional_____
Response Date: __10/19/2017_____

1) What is your official job title? Senior product manager

2) How long have you been in your current role? Four years

3) What attributes or skills helped you to reach your current career level? Master's degree, technical knowledge, quantitative analysis, critical thinking

4) What does your typical day entail? Please, elaborate as much as possible. Meetings, eight to ten hours of meetings; answering phone calls; customer requests

5) How many hours do you work per week? Sixty per week

6) What advice would you give to someone who wants to be in your position someday? Do your work; do it better; do extra; it may not be appreciated at that moment.

7) What has been the role of mentors or coaches in your career advancement? Most of her mentors were developed organically.

8) How many mentors do you have or have you had over your career? Ten to twenty

9) How often do you speak or communicate with your mentor/s? All the time

10) How do you balance your work and life? Don't do it well.

11) How often do you set goals? Daily.

12) What type of goals do you set? Yearly? Monthly? Et cetera? Quarterly, weekly, annually

13) How long have you been working in the market space? Nineteen years

14) What was your first job? Metrics and reporting

15) What valuable lessons have you learned over your career? Be careful what you ask for; all that glitters is not gold.

16) What type of spiritual life do you have? Follower of Jesus Christ

17) Do you attend or engage in any religious activities? Yes, attends church

18) What role has emotional intelligence played in your career progression? Self-control is important, character building.

19) What are some unwritten rules or norms that you learned from being in a white-collar environment? There are always unwritten documented rules; this affects your promotions.

20) Did your parents or grandparents work in a white-collar setting? Yes or No? Yes

21) Did your parents or grandparents teach you how to navigate a white-collar working environment? Yes

22) What did your parents or grandparents teach you about working in a white-collar environment? Have to do better than them …

23) How did you learn about these unwritten rules and norms (observation, mentors, mistakes)? All of the above

24) Currently, how many individuals do you mentor? None officially, three unofficially

25) How often do you listen or read about successful individuals? Frequently

26) What role has self-talk played in your career success? Most of it has been negative; works to override with positive thoughts.

27) How do you motivate yourself each day? Pictures, "you can do it" affirmations, doesn't want to let down her mom.

28) What are some of your hobbies? Sudoku, wine-tasting

29) Do you believe in the PIE model for career success? Yes

30) How often do you exercise? Two times per week

31) How much time do you take off each year to recharge your batteries? Not enough

32) May I use your name in the book? (keep confidential) NA

33) Whom would you recommend that I interview for this book? NA

CHAPTER 2

SURVEY RESULTS

Blue- to White-Collar Thinking Interview (33 questions)
Send to Reginald Ramsey, PhD, MBA @ HRTC1906@gmail.com
Name:____Black/Female/Executive_____
Response Date: __9/20/2017_____

1) What is your official job title? Director
2) How long have you been in your current role? One year
3) What attributes or skills helped you to reach your current career level? Foresight, decision-making, communications
4) What does your typical day entail? Please, elaborate as much as possible. Resource management, contracts, project work
5) How many hours do you work per week? Fifty-five to sixty hours per week
6) What advice would you give to someone who wants to be in your position someday? Learn the business.
7) What has been the role of mentors or coaches in your career advancement? Got information from them.
8) How many mentors do you have or have you had over your career? Five or fewer
9) How often do you speak or communicate with your mentor/s? Once per week
10) How do you balance your work and life? Single mom, went in early and left early.
11) How often do you set goals? Yearly
12) What type of goals do you set? Yearly? Monthly? Et cetera? Yearly

13) How long have you been working in the market space? Twenty years

14) What was your first job? Financial associate

15) What valuable lessons have you learned over your career? Be true to yourself; trust your gut; speak truth to power.

16) What type of spiritual life do you have? Not where it should be

17) Do you attend or engage in any religious activities? Yes, every Sunday

18) What role has emotional intelligence played in your career progression? Tracks her growth and maturity—in her twenties, honest to a fault; thirties recognized that not everyone wants to hear her; forties became more self-aware.

19) What are some unwritten rules or norms that you learned from being in a white-collar environment? Play a little; learn to give enough of your personal life.

20) Did your parents or grandparents work in a white-collar setting? Yes or No? Father was a blue-collar man.

21) Did your parents or grandparents teach you how to navigate a white-collar working environment? Not necessarily

22) What did your parents or grandparents teach you about working in a white-collar environment? Didn't learn the political game.

23) How did you learn about these unwritten rules and norms (observation, mentors, mistakes)? Observations, peer mentoring

24) Currently, how many individuals do you mentor? Six to seven

25) How often do you listen or read about successful individuals? Not as often

26) What role has self-talk played in your career success? Keep the circle very small.

27) How do you motivate yourself each day? Values, responsibility matters

28) What are some of your hobbies? Sorority, reading, photography

29) Do you believe in the PIE model for career success? Yes, exposure is huge.

30) How often do you exercise? Three days per week

31) How much time do you take off each year to recharge your batteries? Two full weeks to recover

32) May I use your name in the book? (keep confidential) NA

33) Whom would you recommend that I interview for this book? NA

Blue- to White-Collar Thinking Interview (33 questions)

Send to Reginald Ramsey, PhD, MBA @ HRTC1906@gmail.com

Name:_____Black/Female/Professional_____

Response Date: ___9/11/2017_____

1) What is your official job title? Product manager

2) How long have you been in your current role? 2.5 years

3) What attributes or skills helped you to reach your current career level? Tenacity, strong work ethic, experience, education, mentors

4) What does your typical day entail? Please, elaborate as much as possible. Interacting with customers, internal and external training, marketing

5) How many hours do you work per week? Less than fifty hours per week

6) What advice would you give to someone who wants to be in your position someday? Consider the product, get experience, understand the product.

7) What has been the role of mentors or coaches in your career advancement? Helped tremendously, sounding board.

8) How many mentors do you have or have you had over your career? Five mentors

9) How often do you speak or communicate with your mentor/s? It varies, depending on the need.

10) How do you balance your work and life? Just do it; set boundaries; family is important.

11) How often do you set goals? Daily

12) What type of goals do you set? Yearly? Monthly? Et cetera? Daily, monthly, yearly

13) How long have you been working in the market space? Twenty-two years

14) What was your first job? Target

15) What valuable lessons have you learned over your career? Stand up for your belief, integrity is key, don't let others stand in your way.

16) What type of spiritual life do you have? Strong, attends church weekly.

17) Do you attend or engage in any religious activities? Yes

18) What role has emotional intelligence played in your career progression? Huge, helps to read people, better relationships.

19) What are some unwritten rules or norms that you learned from being in a white-collar environment? Never talk about politics, religion, and pay, and don't be friends with coworkers.

20) Did your parents or grandparents work in a white-collar setting? Yes or No? No

21) Did your parents or grandparents teach you how to navigate a white-collar working environment? No

22) What did your parents or grandparents teach you about working in a white-collar environment? Honesty, integrity, strong work ethic

23) How did you learn about these unwritten rules and norms (observation, mentors, mistakes)? All of the above, mentor, mistakes

24) Currently, how many individuals do you mentor? None

25) How often do you listen or read about successful individuals? Weekly

26) What role has self-talk played in your career success?

27) How do you motivate yourself each day? Goals

28) What are some of your hobbies? Reading, baking, exercising

29) Do you believe in the PIE model for career success? First time hearing about it.

30) How often do you exercise? Two to three times per week

31) How much time do you take off each year to recharge your batteries? One full week

32) May I use your name in the book? (keep confidential)

33) Whom would you recommend that I interview for this book?

Blue- to White-Collar Thinking Interview (33 questions)

Send to Reginald Ramsey, PhD, MBA @ HRTC1906@gmail.com

Name:_____White/Male/Executive_____

Response Date: ____11/13/2017_____

1) What is your official job title? Director

2) How long have you been in your current role? Two years

3) What attributes or skills helped you to reach your current career level? Technical skills, transferable skills, IT skills, communicate verbally and in written word

4) What does your typical day entail? Please, elaborate as much as possible. Interactions with people, meetings, one-on-one meetings

5) How many hours do you work per week? Fifty per week

6) What advice would you give to someone who wants to be in your position someday? Combined good work and delivery, produce, build relationships with others.

7) What has been the role of mentors or coaches in your career advancement? Important, provided mentorship needed at a particular time, had people to talk to.

8) How many mentors do you have or have you had over your career? Five to ten mentors

9) How often do you speak or communicate with your mentor/s? Monthly

10) How do you balance your work and life? Makes a conscious effort; it is always a challenge.

11) How often do you set goals? Annually

12) What type of goals do you set? Yearly? Monthly? Et cetera? Work and personal

13) How long have you been working in the market space? Twenty-nine years

14) What was your first job? Systems analyst

15) What valuable lessons have you learned over your career? Good work; keep commitments.

16) What type of spiritual life do you have? Rich spiritual life

17) Do you attend or engage in any religious activities? Yes

18) What role has emotional intelligence played in your career progression? Helps with self-awareness; able to read importance of things.

19) What are some unwritten rules or norms that you learned from being in a white-collar environment? Understand expectations.

20) Did your parents or grandparents work in a white-collar setting? Yes or No? No

21) Did your parents or grandparents teach you how to navigate a white-collar working environment? No

22) What did your parents or grandparents teach you about working in a white-collar environment? NA

23) How did you learn about these unwritten rules and norms (observation, mentors, mistakes)? All of the above, adapt and fit in.

24) Currently, how many individuals do you mentor? Five to ten

25) How often do you listen or read about successful individuals? Occasionally

26) What role has self-talk played in your career success? Not a huge role

27) How do you motivate yourself each day? Strong work ethic, commitment, loyalty, accountable for getting things done

28) What are some of your hobbies? Cycling, racketball, photography

29) Do you believe in the PIE model for career success? The key elements

30) How often do you exercise? Regularly with cycling and competitive racketball

31) How much time do you take off each year to recharge your batteries? Two weeks

32) May I use your name in the book? (keep confidential) NA

33) Whom would you recommend that I interview for this book? NA

Blue- to White-Collar Thinking Interview (33 questions)

Send to Reginald Ramsey, PhD, MBA @ HRTC1906@gmail.com

Name:_____Black/Female/Professional_____

Response Date: _____9/13/2017_____

1) What is your official job title? Special claims representative

2) How long have you been in your current role? Twelve years

3) What attributes or skills helped you to reach your current career level? Communications, writing skills, negotiations, analytic

4) What does your typical day entail? Please, elaborate as much as possible. Reading, reports, assessing disabilities, communicating with all parties

5) How many hours do you work per week? Fifty per week

6) What advice would you give to someone who wants to be in your position someday? Have good grasp of English language, writing skills, math skills, college degree

7) What has been the role of mentors or coaches in your career advancement? Always had mentors since high school, helped with advice and referrals

8) How many mentors do you have or have you had over your career? Five or more

9) How often do you speak or communicate with your mentor/s? Once per week

10) How do you balance your work and life? Still trying to learn, organization

11) How often do you set goals? Daily

12) What type of goals do you set? Yearly? Monthly? Et cetera? Yearly

13) How long have you been working in the market space? Thirty-two years

14) What was your first job? Insurance company

15) What valuable lessons have you learned over your career? Be professional all the time; be trustworthy first.

16) What type of spiritual life do you have? Pray with spouse every morning, attend church regularly.

17) Do you attend or engage in any religious activities? Yes

18) What role has emotional intelligence played in your career progression? Big part of her career, helps to deal with all types and walks of life; helps to deal with people after a tragedy.

19) What are some unwritten rules or norms that you learned from being in a white-collar environment? Don't talk politics in the office; dress for success.

20) Did your parents or grandparents work in a white-collar setting? Yes or No? No

21) Did your parents or grandparents teach you how to navigate a white-collar working environment? No

22) What did your parents or grandparents teach you about working in a white-collar environment? NA

23) How did you learn about these unwritten rules and norms (observation, mentors, mistakes)? Observations

24) Currently, how many individuals do you mentor? None

25) How often do you listen or read about successful individuals? Weekly

26) What role has self-talk played in your career success? Big part when stressed ("I can do all things through Christ …")

27) How do you motivate yourself each day? With future goals

28) What are some of your hobbies? Gardening, reading, window shopping ·

29) Do you believe in the PIE model for career success? She would change the model to 70 percent performance in her career.

30) How often do you exercise? Three times per week

31) How much time do you take off each year to recharge your batteries? Three weeks per year

32) May I use your name in the book? (keep confidential) NA

33) Whom would you recommend that I interview for this book? NA

Blue- to White-Collar Thinking Interview (33 questions)
Send to Reginald Ramsey, PhD, MBA @ HRTC1906@gmail.com
Name:_____White/Female/Professional_____
Response Date: ___9/25/2017_____

1) What is your official job title? Consultant
2) How long have you been in your current role? Ten years
3) What attributes or skills helped you to reach your current career level? Knowledge of subject, learned from college and technical school, training, good work ethic, teamwork, and soft skills
4) What does your typical day entail? Please, elaborate as much as possible. Dealing with crisis of the day, emails, influence, strategic planning
5) How many hours do you work per week? Forty to sixty per week
6) What advice would you give to someone who wants to be in your position someday? Have knowledge of the subject matter, talk with people, network, ask for help.
7) What has been the role of mentors or coaches in your career advancement? Have not used them very well. "I didn't ask for help." They can help with understanding and navigating the office politics
8) How many mentors do you have or have you had over your career? Around six
9) How often do you speak or communicate with your mentor/s? Monthly over lunch
10) How do you balance your work and life? As a working mother, it took organization, work from home, leaving early, prioritizing
11) How often do you set goals? A lot, short- and long-term goals
12) What type of goals do you set? Yearly? Monthly? Et cetera? Long and short (monthly goals)
13) How long have you been working in the market space? Forty years
14) What was your first job? University, computer science department

15) What valuable lessons have you learned over your career? Fit into the environment; modify your message as needed.

16) What type of spiritual life do you have? Very spiritual, not religious, respect people, have ethics

17) Do you attend or engage in any religious activities? Went to church, too judgmental

18) What role has emotional intelligence played in your career progression? Very important; helps to work with others; helps to have empathy.

19) What are some unwritten rules or norms that you learned from being in a white-collar environment? Stay away from politics, dress for success, watch how you express your new ideas, don't take the last cup of coffee, fit in your environment.

20) Did your parents or grandparents work in a white-collar setting? Yes or No? No

21) Did your parents or grandparents teach you how to navigate a white-collar working environment? No

22) What did your parents or grandparents teach you about working in a white-collar environment? Insisted on education; work and personal ethics are important.

23) How did you learn about these unwritten rules and norms (observation, mentors, mistakes)? All of the above

24) Currently, how many individuals do you mentor? Two

25) How often do you listen or read about successful individuals? Periodically

26) What role has self-talk played in your career success? A lot, can talk up and down

27) How do you motivate yourself each day? Do the "right thing." Words matter.

28) What are some of your hobbies? Jazzercise, yoga, reading, volunteering

29) Do you believe in the PIE model for career success? I agree. This is how it played out for me. Mentoring is important.

30) How often do you exercise? Jazzercise, two to three times per week

31) How much time do you take off each year to recharge your batteries? Not enough

32) May I use your name in the book? (keep confidential)

33) Whom would you recommend that I interview for this book?

CHAPTER 3

SURVEY RESULTS II

Blue- to White-Collar Thinking Interview (33 questions)
Send to Reginald Ramsey, PhD, MBA @ HRTC1906@gmail.com
Name:____White/Male/Executive_____
Response Date: ____9/27/2017_____

1) What is your official job title? President and CEO
2) How long have you been in your current role? Nine months
3) What attributes or skills helped you to reach your current career level? Broad problem solving, understand people, listening
4) What does your typical day entail? Please, elaborate as much as possible. Early riser, email, follow-up, exercise, meetings
5) How many hours do you work per week? Fifty-five hours per week
6) What advice would you give to someone who wants to be in your position someday? Set high goals, work to achieve them, don't hide from your failures.
7) What has been the role of mentors or coaches in your career advancement? Critical to his success, learned from them.
8) How many mentors do you have or have you had over your career? Too many to count, over twenty
9) How often do you speak or communicate with your mentor/s? Daily, weekly, asked them questions.
10) How do you balance your work and life? Life is about balance; ask his wife and kids.
11) How often do you set goals? Every morning
12) What type of goals do you set? Yearly? Monthly? Et cetera? Daily, and he reassesses them

13) How long have you been working in the market space? Thirty-four years
14) What was your first job? Consulting company
15) What valuable lessons have you learned over your career? Wisdom comes with experience; things looks easy until it is your responsibility.
16) What type of spiritual life do you have? Christian, Lutheran
17) Do you attend or engage in any religious activities? Yes
18) What role has emotional intelligence played in your career progression? Critical role, helps with hiring decisions, recruitment
19) What are some unwritten rules or norms that you learned from being in a white-collar environment? Be observant.
20) Did your parents or grandparents work in a white-collar setting? Yes or No? Mom was a secretary; Dad was a mechanic.
21) Did your parents or grandparents teach you how to navigate a white-collar working environment? No
22) What did your parents or grandparents teach you about working in a white-collar environment? Respect white-collar work.
23) How did you learn about these unwritten rules and norms (observation, mentors, mistakes)? All of the above
24) Currently, how many individuals do you mentor? Ten to fifteen actively
25) How often do you listen or read about successful individuals? A lot, love biographies
26) What role has self-talk played in your career success? High, inner dialogue
27) How do you motivate yourself each day? Burning desire to succeed
28) What are some of your hobbies? Golf, yard work, hunting, fishing, exercise, reading
29) Do you believe in the PIE model for career success? Performance would be higher.
30) How often do you exercise? Daily
31) How much time do you take off each year to recharge your batteries? Two weeks per year
32) May I use your name in the book? (keep confidential) NA
33) Whom would you recommend that I interview for this book?

Blue- to White-Collar Thinking Interview (33 questions)

Send to Reginald Ramsey, PhD, MBA @ HRTC1906@gmail.com

Name:_____Black/Male/Executive_____

Response Date: ___9/14/2017_____

1) What is your official job title? Director

2) How long have you been in your current role? Seven years

3) What attributes or skills helped you to reach your current career level? Problem-solving skills, get results, collaboration

4) What does your typical day entail? Please, elaborate as much as possible. Getting status on a variety of projects, solving problems, prioritize projects

5) How many hours do you work per week? Forty to fifty per week

6) What advice would you give to someone who wants to be in your position someday? Get your credentials, college degrees, find work that you enjoy.

7) What has been the role of mentors or coaches in your career advancement? Mentors provided advice.

8) How many mentors do you have or have you had over your career? Twelve to sixteen direct

9) How often do you speak or communicate with your mentor/s? Weekly

10) How do you balance your work and life? Set an objective for work and life balance.

11) How often do you set goals? Annually

12) What type of goals do you set? Yearly? Monthly? Et cetera? Yearly

13) How long have you been working in the market space? Thirty-seven years

14) What was your first job? In sterile rooms

15) What valuable lessons have you learned over your career? Understand your environment

16) What type of spiritual life do you have? Faith in God

17) Do you attend or engage in any religious activities? Yes

18) What role has emotional intelligence played in your career progression? Very instrumental; helped with his leadership approach, personality; helped to build trust with others.

19) What are some unwritten rules or norms that you learned from being in a white-collar environment? Don't wear emotions on your sleeves; control your emotions; watch for traps and bait; get a mentor.

20) Did your parents or grandparents work in a white-collar setting? Yes or No? No

21) Did your parents or grandparents teach you how to navigate a white-collar working environment? Yes, to some degree, understand the fundamentals.

22) What did your parents or grandparents teach you about working in a white-collar environment? See 21 response.

23) How did you learn about these unwritten rules and norms (observation, mentors, mistakes)? All of the above

24) Currently, how many individuals do you mentor? Four to five now

25) How often do you listen or read about successful individuals? Listened more when he was younger and less experienced on the job.

26) What role has self-talk played in your career success? All the time

27) How do you motivate yourself each day? Understanding his blessing; he is at the "back nine" of his career (soon to retire).

28) What are some of your hobbies? Golf, fishing, board games

29) Do you believe in the PIE model for career success? Yes

30) How often do you exercise? Just started again …

31) How much time do you take off each year to recharge your batteries? Four to five weeks per year

32) May I use your name in the book? (keep confidential) NA

33) Whom would you recommend that I interview for this book? NA

Blue- to White-Collar Thinking Interview (33 questions)

Send to Reginald Ramsey, PhD, MBA @ HRTC1906@gmail.com

Name:_____Black/Male/Executive_____

Response Date: __9/25/2017_____

1) What is your official job title? Director

2) How long have you been in your current role? Four years

3) What attributes or skills helped you to reach your current career level? Technical base, working smarter not harder, get things done

4) What does your typical day entail? Please, elaborate as much as possible. Fitness, phone calls, meetings, daughter to school

5) How many hours do you work per week? Fifty to sixty hours per week

6) What advice would you give to someone who wants to be in your position someday? Stay hungry, have a quest for knowledge.

7) What has been the role of mentors or coaches in your career advancement? Tightly correlated to his success, provides mentorship and sponsorship, provides an advocate.

8) How many mentors do you have or have you had over your career? Multiple

9) How often do you speak or communicate with your mentor/s? Once per month, call or text

10) How do you balance your work and life? By being flexible

11) How often do you set goals? Set career and personal aspirations

12) What type of goals do you set? Yearly? Monthly? Et cetera? Daily

13) How long have you been working in the market space? Twenty-three years

14) What was your first job? Computer guy

15) What valuable lessons have you learned over your career? No one can generate your passion; push through the adversity.

16) What type of spiritual life do you have? Christian

17) Do you attend or engage in any religious activities? Yes

18) What role has emotional intelligence played in your career progression? Helped with his maturity.

19) What are some unwritten rules or norms that you learned from being in a white-collar environment? Male and female likability is key, display competency beyond technical base.

20) Did your parents or grandparents work in a white-collar setting? Yes or No? No

21) Did your parents or grandparents teach you how to navigate a white-collar working environment? No

22) What did your parents or grandparents teach you about working in a white-collar environment? Be respectful, integrity, high work ethic, discipline.

23) How did you learn about these unwritten rules and norms (observation, mentors, mistakes)? Experience, observer

24) Currently, how many individuals do you mentor? Fifteen at work and church

25) How often do you listen or read about successful individuals? On a regular basis

26) What role has self-talk played in your career success? Helps to encourage himself

27) How do you motivate yourself each day? God gave it to him, pay it forward.

28) What are some of your hobbies? Golf, fitness

29) Do you believe in the PIE model for career success? Image is important.

30) How often do you exercise? Five days per week

31) How much time do you take off each year to recharge your batteries? Two to three weeks per year

32) May I use your name in the book? (keep confidential)

33) Whom would you recommend that I interview for this book?

Blue- to White-Collar Thinking Interview (33 questions)

Send to Reginald Ramsey, PhD, MBA @ HRTC1906@gmail.com

Name:_____White/Female/Executive_____

Response Date: _____11/2/2017_____

1) What is your official job title? Vice president

2) How long have you been in your current role? One year

3) What attributes or skills helped you to reach your current career level? Good communication skills, brings people and teams to one goal, critical thinking.

4) What does your typical day entail? Please, elaborate as much as possible. Coaching, mentoring, working with C-level executives

5) How many hours do you work per week? Sixty hours per week

6) What advice would you give to someone who wants to be in your position someday? Don't be afraid to dream big, be yourself, build networks and relationships.

7) What has been the role of mentors or coaches in your career advancement? Very instrumental, can bounce ideas off of them.

8) How many mentors do you have or have you had over your career? Ten to twelve

9) How often do you speak or communicate with your mentor/s? Once per month

10) How do you balance your work and life? Not doing it well, work smarter not harder.

11) How often do you set goals? Every quarter

12) What type of goals do you set? Yearly? Monthly? Et cetera? Personal and group or team goals

13) How long have you been working in the market space? Twenty-six years

14) What was your first job? Art director

15) What valuable lessons have you learned over your career? Make people feel like you are listening, build relationships.

16) What type of spiritual life do you have? Catholic

17) Do you attend or engage in any religious activities? Yes

18) What role has emotional intelligence played in your career progression? Critical, helps to pick up on subtle cues, words matter.

19) What are some unwritten rules or norms that you learned from being in a white-collar environment? Everyone has a vote, golden halo exists for some, learn to work in a consensus environment.

20) Did your parents or grandparents work in a white-collar setting? Yes or No? No

21) Did your parents or grandparents teach you how to navigate a white-collar working environment? No

22) What did your parents or grandparents teach you about working in a white-collar environment? Loyalty, values matter.

23) How did you learn about these unwritten rules and norms (observation, mentors, mistakes)? All of the above

24) Currently, how many individuals do you mentor? Ten direct

25) How often do you listen or read about successful individuals? Once per month

26) What role has self-talk played in your career success? A lot

27) How do you motivate yourself each day? Thank God for everything.

28) What are some of your hobbies? Traveling, hiking, woodworking

29) Do you believe in the PIE model for career success? Agree with the model

30) How often do you exercise? Four times per week

31) How much time do you take off each year to recharge your batteries? Four weeks

32) May I use your name in the book? (keep confidential)

33) Whom would you recommend that I interview for this book?

Blue- to White-Collar Thinking Interview (33 questions)
Send to Reginald Ramsey, PhD, MBA @ HRTC1906@gmail.com
Name:_____Black/Female/Professional_____
Response Date: ____10/13/2017_____

1) What is your official job title? Community development manager
2) How long have you been in your current role? Six months
3) What attributes or skills helped you to reach your current career level? Service, working in marginalized communities
4) What does your typical day entail? Please, elaborate as much as possible. Prayer, emails, understanding current events, meetings (internal and external)
5) How many hours do you work per week? Sixty to seventy per week
6) What advice would you give to someone who wants to be in your position someday? Always realize it is not for self-satisfaction but the growth of others.
7) What has been the role of mentors or coaches in your career advancement? Critical, helps with recommendations, encouragement, challenged her.
8) How many mentors do you have or have you had over your career? Seven formally and fifty plus informally
9) How often do you speak or communicate with your mentor/s? Daily
10) How do you balance your work and life? This is an area of growth.
11) How often do you set goals? Daily
12) What type of goals do you set? Yearly? Monthly? Et cetera? Quarterly, monthly, yearly, and five-year goals
13) How long have you been working in the market space? Twelve years
14) What was your first job? Technical support
15) What valuable lessons have you learned over your career? Never stop learning, connect to others

16) What type of spiritual life do you have? It is everything to her.

17) Do you attend or engage in any religious activities? Yes

18) What role has emotional intelligence played in your career progression? It is a key priority in her life, helps her to stand with moral courage.

19) What are some unwritten rules or norms that you learned from being in a white-collar environment? Mirror your contacts, call with calls, email with emails, no legs exposed, watch your tattoos.

20) Did your parents or grandparents work in a white-collar setting? Yes or No? No

21) Did your parents or grandparents teach you how to navigate a white-collar working environment? Yes

22) What did your parents or grandparents teach you about working in a white-collar environment? Know your environment, know the organizational structure, know the process.

23) How did you learn about these unwritten rules and norms (observation, mentors, mistakes)? All of the above

24) Currently, how many individuals do you mentor? Seven and many informally

25) How often do you listen or read about successful individuals? Very often

26) What role has self-talk played in your career success? Critical

27) How do you motivate yourself each day? Seeing all of my blessings

28) What are some of your hobbies? Art and culture events, music, love outdoors, working out, fitness

29) Do you believe in the PIE model for career success? Yes

30) How often do you exercise? Three to five times per week

31) How much time do you take off each year to recharge your batteries? Three to seven days per quarter

32) May I use your name in the book? (keep confidential)

33) Whom would you recommend that I interview for this book?

Blue- to White-Collar Thinking Interview (33 questions)

Send to Reginald Ramsey, PhD, MBA @ HRTC1906@gmail.com

Name:____Black/Female/Professional_____

Response Date: ___10/10/2017_____

1) What is your official job title? Retail associate (downsized recently)

2) How long have you been in your current role? Eleven months

3) What attributes or skills helped you to reach your current career level? Start with a plan, gather information.

4) What does your typical day entail? Please, elaborate as much as possible. Customer service, dealing with people

5) How many hours do you work per week? Forty to fifty-five per week

6) What advice would you give to someone who wants to be in your position someday? Strive to understand what you want, what are your goals.

7) What has been the role of mentors or coaches in your career advancement? No mentoring relationships

8) How many mentors do you have or have you had over your career? None

9) How often do you speak or communicate with your mentor/s? NA

10) How do you balance your work and life? Make sacrifices for the family

11) How often do you set goals? Every six months

12) What type of goals do you set? Yearly? Monthly? Et cetera? Monthly

13) How long have you been working in the market space? Thirty years

14) What was your first job? Office assistant

15) What valuable lessons have you learned over your career? Don't let other people define you; don't be afraid of change.

16) What type of spiritual life do you have? Growing

17) Do you attend or engage in any religious activities? Yes

18) What role has emotional intelligence played in your career progression? Use it to serve her customers.

19) What are some unwritten rules or norms that you learned from being in a white-collar environment? Understand the exempt versus nonexempt structure.

20) Did your parents or grandparents work in a white-collar setting? Yes or No? No

21) Did your parents or grandparents teach you how to navigate a white-collar working environment? No

22) What did your parents or grandparents teach you about working in a white-collar environment? Nothing

23) How did you learn about these unwritten rules and norms (observation, mentors, mistakes)? Observation

24) Currently, how many individuals do you mentor? Two people

25) How often do you listen or read about successful individuals? Two times per year

26) What role has self-talk played in your career success? Significant part

27) How do you motivate yourself each day? Think about the end goal.

28) What are some of your hobbies? Reading, puzzles

29) Do you believe in the PIE model for career success? Exposure is key.

30) How often do you exercise? Not much

31) How much time do you take off each year to recharge your batteries? Not enough

32) May I use your name in the book? (keep confidential)

33) Whom would you recommend that I interview for this book?

CHAPTER 4

SURVEY RESULTS III

Blue- to White-Collar Thinking Interview (33 questions)

Send to Reginald Ramsey, PhD, MBA @ HRTC1906@gmail.com

Name:_____White/Male/Executive_____

Response Date: ____10/16/2017_____

1) What is your official job title? Vice president
2) How long have you been in your current role? Ten years
3) What attributes or skills helped you to reach your current career level? Education, MBA degree, job experience
4) What does your typical day entail? Please, elaborate as much as possible. Early work, emails, meetings, presenting at meetings, leading meetings
5) How many hours do you work per week? Fifty-five to sixty hours per week
6) What advice would you give to someone who wants to be in your position someday? Balance, "Are you willing to make the sacrifice?"
7) What has been the role of mentors or coaches in your career advancement? Had role models.
8) How many mentors do you have or have you had over your career? Several role models, leveraged his role models.
9) How often do you speak or communicate with your mentor/s? Depended on the situation
10) How do you balance your work and life? By trying to exercise, run, other stress relievers, vacations with family
11) How often do you set goals? Monthly

12) What type of goals do you set? Yearly? Monthly? Et cetera? Monthly, quarterly, yearly (reassess)

13) How long have you been working in the market space? Forty-five years

14) What was your first job? Systems analyst

15) What valuable lessons have you learned over your career? People can be nasty; people have agendas; don't be naïve to that.

16) What type of spiritual life do you have? Catholic

17) Do you attend or engage in any religious activities? Yes

18) What role has emotional intelligence played in your career progression? Helped him to have empathy for others, think from others' perspective.

19) What are some unwritten rules or norms that you learned from being in a white-collar environment? There are consequences for not following the "unwritten" rules.

20) Did your parents or grandparents work in a white-collar setting? Yes or No? No

21) Did your parents or grandparents teach you how to navigate a white-collar working environment? No

22) What did your parents or grandparents teach you about working in a white-collar environment? Work ethic is key.

23) How did you learn about these unwritten rules and norms (observation, mentors, mistakes)? Work ethic

24) Currently, how many individuals do you mentor? Two to five

25) How often do you listen or read about successful individuals? Not much

26) What role has self-talk played in your career success? Helped with his success

27) How do you motivate yourself each day? Excited about the work

28) What are some of your hobbies? Working out and running

29) Do you believe in the PIE model for career success? Yes, absolutely.

30) How often do you exercise? Often

31) How much time do you take off each year to recharge your batteries? Two weeks and holidays

32) May I use your name in the book? (keep confidential)

33) Whom would you recommend that I interview for this book?

Blue- to White-Collar Thinking Interview (33 questions)

Send to Reginald Ramsey, PhD, MBA @ HRTC1906@gmail.com

Name:____White/Male/Executive_____

Response Date: ___9/21/2017_____

1) What is your official job title? Director

2) How long have you been in your current role? Eight years

3) What attributes or skills helped you to reach your current career level? Positive attitude, interpersonal skills, project management

4) What does your typical day entail? Please, elaborate as much as possible. Meetings, one-on-one meetings, project meetings

5) How many hours do you work per week? Sixty hours per week and on the weekends

6) What advice would you give to someone who wants to be in your position someday? Figure out your passion.

7) What has been the role of mentors or coaches in your career advancement? Provide sponsorship.

8) How many mentors do you have or have you had over your career? Twelve to eighteen

9) How often do you speak or communicate with your mentor/s? Once per month

10) How do you balance your work and life? Focus on the outcome, varied at different points in his life.

11) How often do you set goals? Weekly, daily

12) What type of goals do you set? Yearly? Monthly? Et cetera? Daily, monthly, yearly

13) How long have you been working in the market space? Twenty-six years

14) What was your first job? Systems programmer

15) What valuable lessons have you learned over your career? Be clear about what you want; take control over your career; articulate it to your mentors and sponsors.

16) What type of spiritual life do you have? Out of balance, used to attend church

17) Do you attend or engage in any religious activities? Yes

18) What role has emotional intelligence played in your career progression? Very important, self-regulation, self-awareness

19) What are some unwritten rules or norms that you learned from being in a white-collar environment? Be aware of the politics. Don't be political. Don't speak about others behind their backs. Everyone knows something.

20) Did your parents or grandparents work in a white-collar setting? Yes or No? No, Grandfather was white-collar worker (not a corp guy).

21) Did your parents or grandparents teach you how to navigate a white-collar working environment? No

22) What did your parents or grandparents teach you about working in a white-collar environment? Get mentors.

23) How did you learn about these unwritten rules and norms (observation, mentors, mistakes)? All of the above

24) Currently, how many individuals do you mentor? Twelve to twenty-five, depends

25) How often do you listen or read about successful individuals? Don't read much; will listen to successful books on CD or tape.

26) What role has self-talk played in your career success? Uses positive self-talk to motivate himself during the tough periods.

27) How do you motivate yourself each day? Start and reset; get some momentum.

28) What are some of your hobbies? Woodwork, jog, yard, computer technology

29) Do you believe in the PIE model for career success? True

30) How often do you exercise? Every day

31) How much time do you take off each year to recharge your batteries? Several weeks per year

32) May I use your name in the book? (keep confidential)

33) Whom would you recommend that I interview for this book?

Blue- to White-Collar Thinking Interview (33 questions)

Send to Reginald Ramsey, PhD, MBA @ HRTC1906@gmail.com

Name:_____Black/Male/Executive_____

Response Date: ____10/20/2017_____

1) What is your official job title? Founder, principle solution architect

2) How long have you been in your current role? Two years

3) What attributes or skills helped you to reach your current career level? Strategic thinking, process development, communication skills (verbal and written)

4) What does your typical day entail? Please, elaborate as much as possible. Work out, eat right, business development, follow up on leads, customer meetings

5) How many hours do you work per week? Fifty to sixty per week

6) What advice would you give to someone who wants to be in your position someday? Prepare your heart and mind; be clear and self-aware.

7) What has been the role of mentors or coaches in your career advancement? Key, need more, critical, coaching

8) How many mentors do you have or have you had over your career? Four to seven mentors

9) How often do you speak or communicate with your mentor/s? Monthly

10) How do you balance your work and life? Clear Saturdays and weekday evenings

11) How often do you set goals? Quarterly, daily

12) What type of goals do you set? Yearly? Monthly? Et cetera? Quarterly, daily

13) How long have you been working in the market space? Thirteen years

14) What was your first job? Information analyst

15) What valuable lessons have you learned over your career? Stay in the driver's seat; you are the asset; invest in yourself.

16) What type of spiritual life do you have? Needs to work on his prayer life.

17) Do you attend or engage in any religious activities? Yes

18) What role has emotional intelligence played in your career progression? Self-awareness, pick up on social cues.

19) What are some unwritten rules or norms that you learned from being in a white-collar environment? PIE; always know your audience; don't outshine.

20) Did your parents or grandparents work in a white-collar setting? Yes or No? Yes

21) Did your parents or grandparents teach you how to navigate a white-collar working environment? Yes

22) What did your parents or grandparents teach you about working in a white-collar environment? Politics in the workplace, what factors are important, image and exposure.

23) How did you learn about these unwritten rules and norms (observation, mentors, mistakes)? All of the above

24) Currently, how many individuals do you mentor? None

25) How often do you listen or read about successful individuals? Every day

26) What role has self-talk played in your career success? Accept faith; reject fear.

27) How do you motivate yourself each day? Caffeine, James Brown, men in the Bible

28) What are some of your hobbies? Foodie, sports, working out

29) Do you believe in the PIE model for career success? Yes

30) How often do you exercise? Five times per week

31) How much time do you take off each year to recharge your batteries? One to two weeks per year

32) May I use your name in the book? (keep confidential)

33) Whom would you recommend that I interview for this book?

Blue- to White-Collar Thinking Interview (33 questions)
Send to Reginald Ramsey, PhD, MBA @ HRTC1906@gmail.com
Name:_____Black/Female/Professional_____
Response Date: _____9/25/2017_____

1) What is your official job title? Medical nurse
2) How long have you been in your current role? Eight years
3) What attributes or skills helped you to reach your current career level? Persistence, willpower, self-drive, motivation, never being content
4) What does your typical day entail? Please, elaborate as much as possible. Patients, checking on patients, thorough assessments
5) How many hours do you work per week? Forty-eight hours per week
6) What advice would you give to someone who wants to be in your position someday? Think about your career or job
7) What has been the role of mentors or coaches in your career advancement? Helped her to stay on track; provided innovative ideas.
8) How many mentors do you have or have you had over your career? About six mentors
9) How often do you speak or communicate with your mentor/s? Monthly
10) How do you balance your work and life? Calendar, write down everything on paper
11) How often do you set goals? Daily
12) What type of goals do you set? Yearly? Monthly? Et cetera? Daily
13) How long have you been working in the market space? Twenty-five years
14) What was your first job? Manager at fast-food restaurant
15) What valuable lessons have you learned over your career? Patience, communication, cooperation
16) What type of spiritual life do you have? Pray daily, mediate daily
17) Do you attend or engage in any religious activities? Every now and then

18) What role has emotional intelligence played in your career progression? Compassion for human beings

19) What are some unwritten rules or norms that you learned from being in a white-collar environment? Be a good listener; learn to follow before you lead.

20) Did your parents or grandparents work in a white-collar setting? Yes or No? No

21) Did your parents or grandparents teach you how to navigate a white-collar working environment? No

22) What did your parents or grandparents teach you about working in a white-collar environment? Persistence; don't give up; no mountain is too high to climb.

23) How did you learn about these unwritten rules and norms (observation, mentors, mistakes)? All of the above

24) Currently, how many individuals do you mentor? Three individuals

25) How often do you listen or read about successful individuals? Every day

26) What role has self-talk played in your career success? Big role, it must come from within to reflect out …

27) How do you motivate yourself each day? Pray; tell myself, "What can I learn today?"; self-talk.

28) What are some of your hobbies? Reading, gardening, cooking, community service

29) Do you believe in the PIE model for career success? I agree. Who you know is important.

30) How often do you exercise? Every day, walking

31) How much time do you take off each year to recharge your batteries? Three weeks

32) May I use your name in the book? (keep confidential)

33) Whom would you recommend that I interview for this book?

Blue- to White-Collar Thinking Interview (33 questions)

Send to Reginald Ramsey, PhD, MBA @ HRTC1906@gmail.com

Name:_____Black/Male/Professional_____

Response Date: ___9/28/2017_____

1) What is your official job title? Senior IT project manager

2) How long have you been in your current role? Seven months

3) What attributes or skills helped you to reach your current career level? Determination and mentorship

4) What does your typical day entail? Please, elaborate as much as possible. Prioritization, planning, people conflicts, anticipating management expectations

5) How many hours do you work per week? Forty to fifty hours per week

6) What advice would you give to someone who wants to be in your position someday? Do your homework; find your way to get experience.

7) What has been the role of mentors or coaches in your career advancement? Huge, would not have advanced.

8) How many mentors do you have or have you had over your career? Twelve to fifteen mentors

9) How often do you speak or communicate with your mentor/s? Monthly

10) How do you balance your work and life? Prioritize

11) How often do you set goals? Weekly

12) What type of goals do you set? Yearly? Monthly? Et cetera? Weekly

13) How long have you been working in the market space? Fourteen years

14) What was your first job? Computer programmer

15) What valuable lessons have you learned over your career? You don't have to have all of the answers.

16) What type of spiritual life do you have? Acknowledge God; his son, Jesus.

17) Do you attend or engage in any religious activities? Yes

18) What role has emotional intelligence played in your career progression? Helps to form and keep relationships.

19) What are some unwritten rules or norms that you learned from being in a white-collar environment? Ask questions, network, have a sense of urgency.

20) Did your parents or grandparents work in a white-collar setting? Yes or No? No

21) Did your parents or grandparents teach you how to navigate a white-collar working environment? No

22) What did your parents or grandparents teach you about working in a white-collar environment? Work hard, work harder as a black man.

23) How did you learn about these unwritten rules and norms (observation, mentors, mistakes)? All of the above

24) Currently, how many individuals do you mentor? Ten individuals

25) How often do you listen or read about successful individuals? Monthly

26) What role has self-talk played in your career success? Critical, what you say to yourself will come true.

27) How do you motivate yourself each day? Finding opportunities to get better

28) What are some of your hobbies? Music (DJ), cooking, hosting friends and family

29) Do you believe in the PIE model for career success? Yes, branding is key.

30) How often do you exercise? Five times per week

31) How much time do you take off each year to recharge your batteries? Four weeks

32) May I use your name in the book? (keep confidential)

33) Whom would you recommend that I interview for this book?

Blue- to White-Collar Thinking Interview (33 questions)

Send to Reginald Ramsey, PhD, MBA @ HRTC1906@gmail.com

Name:_____Black/Female/Manager_____

Response Date: __11/9/2017 and 1/4/2018_____

1) What is your official job title? IT manager

2) How long have you been in your current role? Four years

3) What attributes or skills helped you to reach your current career level? Faith, family, level of commitment

4) What does your typical day entail? Please, elaborate as much as possible. Understanding priorities for day and beyond

5) How many hours do you work per week? Sixty hours per week

6) What advice would you give to someone who wants to be in your position someday? Money and title is not enough; put your heart in it.

7) What has been the role of mentors or coaches in your career advancement? Effective mentors push you, make you stretch.

8) How many mentors do you have or have you had over your career? Ten to twenty mentors

9) How often do you speak or communicate with your mentor/s? Monthly/quarterly, depends on the mentor and what he or she brings to the table.

10) How do you balance your work and life? Make conscious choices.

11) How often do you set goals? Regularly

12) What type of goals do you set? Yearly? Monthly? Et cetera? Family, church, community, et cetera.

13) How long have you been working in the market space? Twenty-eight years

14) What was your first job? Engineer

15) What valuable lessons have you learned over your career? Prayer is the key; need sponsors and mentors and advocates to succeed.

16) What type of spiritual life do you have? She believes and trusts in God.

17) Do you attend or engage in any religious activities? Yes

18) What role has emotional intelligence played in your career progression? Area of growth for her; use as a tool.

19) What are some unwritten rules or norms that you learned from being in a white-collar environment? Understand the meeting before the meeting, who has the power of influence; build a relationship beforehand.

20) Did your parents or grandparents work in a white-collar setting? Yes or No? No

21) Did your parents or grandparents teach you how to navigate a white-collar working environment? Yes

22) What did your parents or grandparents teach you about working in a white-collar environment? Don't forget where you come from; respect will open doors; maintain respect for others and yourself.

23) How did you learn about these unwritten rules and norms (observation, mentors, mistakes)? All of the above

24) Currently, how many individuals do you mentor? Three individuals

25) How often do you listen or read about successful individuals? Daily

26) What role has self-talk played in your career success? Leverage

27) How do you motivate yourself each day? Prayer

28) What are some of your hobbies? Reading, watching sports

29) Do you believe in the PIE model for career success? Yes

30) How often do you exercise? Not often, rarely

31) How much time do you take off each year to recharge your batteries? Two weeks

32) May I use your name in the book? (keep confidential)

33) Whom would you recommend that I interview for this book?

Blue- to White-Collar Thinking Interview (33 questions)
Send to Reginald Ramsey, PhD, MBA @ HRTC1906@gmail.com
Name:_____White/Male/Executive_____
Response Date: ____9/19/2017_____

1) What is your official job title? President/owner

2) How long have you been in your current role? Twelve years

3) What attributes or skills helped you to reach your current career level? Hard work, leadership, business acumen

4) What does your typical day entail? Please, elaborate as much as possible. Business development, execution of business, administration of business

5) How many hours do you work per week? Sixty to eighty hours per week

6) What advice would you give to someone who wants to be in your position someday? Concentrate on your attributes; get results.

7) What has been the role of mentors or coaches in your career advancement? Crucial, couldn't have done it without them.

8) How many mentors do you have or have you had over your career? Twenty-five to thirty mentors

9) How often do you speak or communicate with your mentor/s? When I needed to, often

10) How do you balance your work and life? Have a wonderful spouse

11) How often do you set goals? Daily

12) What type of goals do you set? Yearly? Monthly? Et cetera? Daily

13) How long have you been working in the market space? Forty-five years

14) What was your first job? Technical support person

15) What valuable lessons have you learned over your career? Have ethics and respect for others.

16) What type of spiritual life do you have? Very strong and deep

17) Do you attend or engage in any religious activities? Yes

18) What role has emotional intelligence played in your career progression? Good communications, empathy, self-regulation

19) What are some unwritten rules or norms that you learned from being in a white-collar environment? Integrity is important; demand it of yourself.

20) Did your parents or grandparents work in a white-collar setting? Yes or No? No

21) Did your parents or grandparents teach you how to navigate a white-collar working environment? No

22) What did your parents or grandparents teach you about working in a white-collar environment? Be polite, say please and thank you, be respectful.

23) How did you learn about these unwritten rules and norms (observation, mentors, mistakes)? All of the above

24) Currently, how many individuals do you mentor? Five students

25) How often do you listen or read about successful individuals? A lot

26) What role has self-talk played in your career success? Talks to himself a lot.

27) How do you motivate yourself each day? By saying thanks every day …

28) What are some of your hobbies? Weight-lifting, school, welding

29) Do you believe in the PIE model for career success? Disagree

30) How often do you exercise? Every day

31) How much time do you take off each year to recharge your batteries? Very seldom

32) May I use your name in the book? (keep confidential)

33) Whom would you recommend that I interview for this book?

CHAPTER 5

SURVEY RESULTS IV

Blue- to White-Collar Thinking Interview (33 questions)

Send to Reginald Ramsey, PhD, MBA @ HRTC1906@gmail.com

Name:____White/Female/Executive_____

Response Date: __9/20/2017_____

1) What is your official job title? Senior director

2) How long have you been in your current role? Three years

3) What attributes or skills helped you to reach your current career level? Get things done, teamwork, leadership

4) What does your typical day entail? Please, elaborate as much as possible. Coaching, meetings

5) How many hours do you work per week? Fifty to fifty-five per week

6) What advice would you give to someone who wants to be in your position someday? Technical knowledge is important; soft skills are key; develop your people skills.

7) What has been the role of mentors or coaches in your career advancement? Helps to address questions.

8) How many mentors do you have or have you had over your career? Six to ten mentors

9) How often do you speak or communicate with your mentor/s? Weekly

10) How do you balance your work and life? Use a tribe method; used other moms to help her with kids.

11) How often do you set goals? Annually

12) What type of goals do you set? Yearly? Monthly? Et cetera? Yearly

13) How long have you been working in the market space? Forty years

14) What was your first job? City planner

15) What valuable lessons have you learned over your career? You don't get anything done by yourself; hard work won't always get recognized.

16) What type of spiritual life do you have? Strong faith

17) Do you attend or engage in any religious activities? Yes

18) What role has emotional intelligence played in your career progression? Biggest strength

19) What are some unwritten rules or norms that you learned from being in a white-collar environment? No tattoos, appropriate dress, no low cut, too tight is bad, watch your weight.

20) Did your parents or grandparents work in a white-collar setting? Yes or No? Yes

21) Did your parents or grandparents teach you how to navigate a white-collar working environment? No

22) What did your parents or grandparents teach you about working in a white-collar environment? Nothing

23) How did you learn about these unwritten rules and norms (observation, mentors, mistakes)? All of the above

24) Currently, how many individuals do you mentor? Three to four individuals

25) How often do you listen or read about successful individuals? Read about people from time to time

26) What role has self-talk played in your career success? Not as much as it should; gives herself pep talks.

27) How do you motivate yourself each day? Influence junkie, likes to influence the decision-making process.

28) What are some of your hobbies? Exercise, reading

29) Do you believe in the PIE model for career success? Yes

30) How often do you exercise? Three times per week

31) How much time do you take off each year to recharge your batteries? Two weeks per year

32) May I use your name in the book? (keep confidential)

33) Whom would you recommend that I interview for this book?

Blue- to White-Collar Thinking Interview (33 questions)
Send to Reginald Ramsey, PhD, MBA @ HRTC1906@gmail.com
Name:_____Black, Female, Professional_____
Response Date: ____9/19/2017_____

1) What is your official job title? Project manager
2) How long have you been in your current role? Fifteen years
3) What attributes or skills helped you to reach your current career level? Determination, planning, working with others; motivated
4) What does your typical day entail? Please, elaborate as much as possible. Meetings, communicating, status updates, vendor management, problem identification
5) How many hours do you work per week? Fifty to fifty-five hours per week
6) What advice would you give to someone who wants to be in your position someday? Education, lifelong learning, project management
7) What has been the role of mentors or coaches in your career advancement? Provided technical guidance; helped to open her eyes to other types of work and work areas.
8) How many mentors do you have or have you had over your career? Two to six business mentors
9) How often do you speak or communicate with your mentor/s? Bimonthly or monthly, it depended on the situation.
10) How do you balance your work and life? Prioritize things; workaholic—need to work on this area.
11) How often do you set goals? Once per year
12) What type of goals do you set? Yearly? Monthly? Et cetera? Yearly
13) How long have you been working in the market space? Thirty years
14) What was your first job? Programmer

15) What valuable lessons have you learned over your career? Be patient.

16) What type of spiritual life do you have? Attend church; pray every day and throughout the day.

17) Do you attend or engage in any religious activities? Yes, church.

18) What role has emotional intelligence played in your career progression? Helped her to be more pragmatic and rational; less finger-pointing; understand both sides (vendors versus company).

19) What are some unwritten rules or norms that you learned from being in a white-collar environment? It's not always about the work; it's about who you know.

20) Did your parents or grandparents work in a white-collar setting? Yes or No? No, factory workers

21) Did your parents or grandparents teach you how to navigate a white-collar working environment? No, instilled some good values (e.g., loyalty).

22) What did your parents or grandparents teach you about working in a white-collar environment? Loyalty; work every day; do your job.

23) How did you learn about these unwritten rules and norms (observation, mentors, mistakes)? All of the above, mostly mistakes

24) Currently, how many individuals do you mentor? None, still have small children at home.

25) How often do you listen or read about successful individuals? All the time—radio stations, reading, love to read

26) What role has self-talk played in your career success? Helps to think about things; play out in her mind.

27) How do you motivate yourself each day? Enjoy what she does; comes naturally; talks to herself (focus on the future).

28) What are some of your hobbies? Exercise, shop, travel, reading, family activities

29) Do you believe in the PIE model for career success? Think it exists; it's reality.
30) How often do you exercise? Three times per week
31) How much time do you take off each year to recharge your batteries? Four weeks
32) May I use your name in the book? (keep confidential) NA
33) Whom would you recommend that I interview for this book?

Blue- to White-Collar Thinking Interview (33 questions)
Send to Reginald Ramsey, PhD, MBA @ HRTC1906@gmail.com
Name:_____Black, Female, Professional_____
Response Date: ____9/18/2017_____

1) What is your official job title? Technical project manager

2) How long have you been in your current role? Two months

3) What attributes or skills helped you to reach your current career level? Attention to details, tenacity, focus, empathy, people skills

4) What does your typical day entail? Please, elaborate as much as possible. Project-based work, get information, give information, direct vendors

5) How many hours do you work per week? Forty to fifty hours per week

6) What advice would you give to someone who wants to be in your position someday? Set goals; review your goals weekly, monthly, and yearly; get a mentor.

7) What has been the role of mentors or coaches in your career advancement? Helped to correct some habits; helped with work transition.

8) How many mentors do you have or have you had over your career? Three to four mentors

9) How often do you speak or communicate with your mentor/s? Biweekly and monthly

10) How do you balance your work and life? Take breaks; address toxic managers with an exit strategy; make healthy choices; manage stress; network with other groups outside of work.

11) How often do you set goals? Quarterly

12) What type of goals do you set? Yearly? Monthly? Et cetera? Quarterly

13) How long have you been working in the market space? Twelve years

14) What was your first job? Computer technician

15) What valuable lessons have you learned over your career? Soft skills are important.

16) What type of spiritual life do you have? Not a religious person, Christian, Prayed up

17) Do you attend or engage in any religious activities? Two times per year; pray for right path

18) What role has emotional intelligence played in your career progression? Most important piece; helps to separate her from her peers; she's able to handle stress; can keep secrets; her best asset.

19) What are some unwritten rules or norms that you learned from being in a white-collar environment? People carry their problems with them; don't take anything personally; learn to engage in small talk.

20) Did your parents or grandparents work in a white-collar setting? Yes or No? Yes, father was blue collar with no degree; he networked with others.

21) Did your parents or grandparents teach you how to navigate a white-collar working environment? They tried in their own way. They didn't have a blueprint to follow.

22) What did your parents or grandparents teach you about working in a white-collar environment? Networking is important.

23) How did you learn about these unwritten rules and norms (observation, mentors, mistakes)? All of the above; observed her father go through the transition.

24) Currently, how many individuals do you mentor? No formal mentees yet

25) How often do you listen or read about successful individuals? Not been doing this activity

26) What role has self-talk played in your career success? Helps her to think; internal coach; helps her to get through the day; have conversations with herself.

27) How do you motivate yourself each day? Project oriented; see everything as a project.

28) What are some of your hobbies? Jazz music; love to listen to music

29) Do you believe in the PIE model for career success? Yes, goes back to technical skills only 10 percent of her success; exposure was important to her career advancement.

30) How often do you exercise? Three to four times per week

31) How much time do you take off each year to recharge your batteries? Not enough, about four days; need to work on this area.

32) May I use your name in the book? (keep confidential) NA

33) Whom would you recommend that I interview for this book? Will provide some names

Blue- to White-Collar Thinking Interview (33 questions)

Send to Reginald Ramsey, PhD, MBA @ HRTC1906@gmail.com

Name:__White, Male, Executive_____

Response Date: ____9/13/2017_____

1) What is your official job title? Director

2) How long have you been in your current role? Two years

3) What attributes or skills helped you to reach your current career level? Relentless pursuit of education, certifications, master's degree

4) What does your typical day entail? Please, elaborate as much as possible.

    Meeting with leadership team; helping to clarify what to achieve; manage the "whirlwind."

5) How many hours do you work per week? Forty-five hours per week

6) What advice would you give to someone who wants to be in your position someday? Figure out your passion, what makes you happy.

7) What has been the role of mentors or coaches in your career advancement? Mentors played a major role in my career advancement; get more than one mentor.

8) How many mentors do you have or have you had over your career? One formal mentor, six to ten informal mentors

9) How often do you speak or communicate with your mentor/s? Daily

10) How do you balance your work and life? Made a choice not to work the fifty to sixty hours per week; prioritize; take vacations.

11) How often do you set goals? On a regular basis; I am goals driven

12) What type of goals do you set? Yearly? Monthly? Et cetera? Monthly

13) How long have you been working in the market space? Twenty-nine years

14) What was your first job? Systems analyst

15) What valuable lessons have you learned over your career? Go with your passion; shoot two levels above; give back to society.

16) What type of spiritual life do you have? Active Christian

17) Do you attend or engage in any religious activities? Yes

18) What role has emotional intelligence played in your career progression? Played a major role.

19) What are some unwritten rules or norms that you learned from being in a white-collar environment? Attire matters; learn to network; build relationships; create demand for yourself.

20) Did your parents or grandparents work in a white-collar setting? Yes or No? No, both of them were blue-collar workers.

21) Did your parents or grandparents teach you how to navigate a white-collar working environment? No

22) What did your parents or grandparents teach you about working in a white-collar environment? Don't recall.

23) How did you learn about these unwritten rules and norms (observation, mentors, mistakes)? All of the above

24) Currently, how many individuals do you mentor? Informally a few

25) How often do you listen or read about successful individuals? On a regular basis

26) What role has self-talk played in your career success? Major role

27) How do you motivate yourself each day? Start with a love of my job and career.

28) What are some of your hobbies? Fitness, running, triathelete, scuba diving

29) Do you believe in the PIE model for career success? Yes

30) How often do you exercise? Regularly

31) How much time do you take off each year to recharge your batteries? Six and a half weeks

32) May I use your name in the book? (keep confidential) NA

33) Whom would you recommend that I interview for this book? NA

Blue- to White-Collar Thinking Interview (33 questions)

Send to Reginald Ramsey, PhD, MBA @ HRTC1906@gmail.com

Name:_____Black, Male, Professional__

Response Date: ___9/14/2017__

1) What is your official job title? Program manager

2) How long have you been in your current role? Fourteen months

3) What attributes or skills helped you to reach your current career levels? Education, boldness, determination, willing to learn, willing to take risks

4) What does your typical day entail? Please, elaborate as much as possible. Responding to customers, managing programs, many meetings internally and externally

5) How many hours do you work per week? Fifty-five to sixty hours per week

6) What advice would you give to someone who wants to be in your position someday? Get a great education; develop a passion for learning.

7) What has been the role of mentors or coaches in your career advancement? Significant, they helped me to understand the white-collar game!

8) How many mentors do you have or have you had over your career? Over twenty-five or more

9) How often do you speak or communicate with your mentor/s? Varied—some monthly, some weekly, some quarterly

10) How do you balance your work and life? Prioritize my family over work

11) How often do you set goals? Daily

12) What type of goals do you set? Yearly? Monthly? Et cetera? Daily, monthly, yearly, five-year, fifteen-year

13) How long have you been working in the market space? Thirty years

14) What was your first job? Senior technical associate

15) What valuable lessons have you learned over your career? There is power in giving to others and power in taking risks.

16) What type of spiritual life do you have? Very deep faith in Jesus Christ; have a personal relationship with Christ.

17) Do you attend or engage in any religious activities? Yes, attend church on a regular basis.

18) What role has emotional intelligence played in your career progression? Significant, helped me to control my anger and temper; learned how to breathe and discuss difficult issues without becoming disagreeable. Learned how to get along with different people who may be hard to get along with.

19) What are some unwritten rules or norms that you learned from being in a white-collar environment? Dress code is important; facial hair is not accepted in some corporate settings.

20) Did your parents or grandparents work in a white-collar setting? Yes or No? No

21) Did your parents or grandparents teach you how to navigate a white-collar working environment? No. They were not exposed to the white-collar working environment.

22) What did your parents or grandparents teach you about working in a white-collar environment? Do a good job; people will see it; you will get rewarded. (This is not the case.)

23) How did you learn about these unwritten rules and norms (observation, mentors, mistakes)? Observations, mentors, coaches, managers, and mistakes

24) Currently, how many individuals do you mentor? Six to ten individuals

25) How often do you listen or read about successful individuals? Daily

26) What role has self-talk played in your career success? Significant; I talk to myself daily.

27) How do you motivate yourself each day? By my willingness to serve God, serving others

28) What are some of your hobbies? Golf, tennis, chess, fishing, traveling

29) Do you believe in the PIE model for career success? Yes, it helped to advance my career to the next level.

30) How often do you exercise? Daily

31) How much time do you take off each year to recharge your batteries? Four weeks per year

32) May I use your name in the book? (keep confidential) NA

33) Whom would you recommend that I interview for this book? Spouse

CHAPTER 6

SURVEY RESULTS V

Blue- to White-Collar Thinking Interview (33 questions)
Send to Reginald Ramsey, PhD, MBA @ HRTC1906@gmail.com
Name:_____Black, Male, Manager_____
Response Date: _____9/13/2017_____

1) What is your official job title? Manager
2) How long have you been in your current role? Fifteen years
3) What attributes or skills helped you to reach your current career level? Analytical, written skills, responsiveness to others
4) What does your typical day entail? Please, elaborate as much as possible. Analyzing, real estate transactions, writing deal memoranda
5) How many hours do you work per week? Fifty hours per week
6) What advice would you give to someone who wants to be in your position someday? Strong math skills, writing skills, people skills
7) What has been the role of mentors or coaches in your career advancement? Always had mentors; had good bosses.
8) How many mentors do you have or have you had over your career? Approximately three
9) How often do you speak or communicate with your mentor/s? Two to three times per week
10) How do you balance your work and life? Separate work from home
11) How often do you set goals? Annually; review twice per year
12) What type of goals do you set? Yearly? Monthly? Et cetera? Yearly
13) How long have you been working in the market space? Twenty-nine years

14) What was your first job? Engineer

15) What valuable lessons have you learned over your career? Meet your commitments; "keep your word"; do what you say you are going to do; have a good work ethic

16) What type of spiritual life do you have? Prays with spouse daily; attends church; attends Bible study from time to time.

17) Do you attend or engage in any religious activities? Yes

18) What role has emotional intelligence played in your career progression? It was key to his career; helped him to learn how to socialize and take care of business, not burden people with his problems, not to "overshare" information.

19) What are some unwritten rules or norms that you learned from being in a white-collar environment? Don't overshare personal information; be good at golf.

20) Did your parents or grandparents work in a white-collar setting? Yes or No? No

21) Did your parents or grandparents teach you how to navigate a white-collar working environment? Yes, Mom and Dad taught him to meet commitments, work hard.

22) What did your parents or grandparents teach you about working in a white-collar environment? See 21.

23) How did you learn about these unwritten rules and norms (observation, mentors, mistakes)? Observations and mentors

24) Currently, how many individuals do you mentor? One informally

25) How often do you listen or read about successful individuals? Infrequently, not that often

26) What role has self-talk played in your career success? Big role; prays at desk; helps to manage stress; provides self-affirmation.

27) How do you motivate yourself each day? Loves his job; likes the people he works with.

28) What are some of your hobbies? Golf, puzzles, sudoku, Las Vegas, nightlife, gaming tables

29) Do you believe in the PIE model for career success? Yes, exposure is key.

30) How often do you exercise? Daily

31) How much time do you take off each year to recharge your batteries? Three to four weeks

32) May I use your name in the book? (keep confidential) NA

33) Whom would you recommend that I interview for this book? NA

Blue- to White-Collar Thinking Interview (33 questions)

Send to Reginald Ramsey, PhD, MBA @ HRTC1906@gmail.com

Name:___White/Male/Executive (military to civilian)_____

Response Date: ____9/29/2017_

1) What is your official job title? Director

2) How long have you been in your current role? Six months

3) What attributes or skills helped you to reach your current career level? Tenacity; wrote out his goals; goals were three, five, and ten years.

4) What does your typical day entail? Please, elaborate as much as possible. Working with internal leadership team, planning, contract review, meetings

5) How many hours do you work per week? Fifty to sixty per week

6) What advice would you give to someone who wants to be in your position someday? Have a passion for the content; be interested in people and relationships; ensure others' needs are met; be transparent.

7) What has been the role of mentors or coaches in your career advancement? Pivotal; mentors tell you what you need to hear; you need their feedback to grow and adjust your behavior.

8) How many mentors do you have or have you had over your career? Six really good mentors

9) How often do you speak or communicate with your mentor/s? Had monthly conversations; was able to pick up the phone and call a mentor anytime.

10) How do you balance your work and life? Do not work on the weekends.

11) How often do you set goals? Three, five, and ten years; reset on an annual basis.

12) What type of goals do you set? Yearly? Monthly? Et cetera? See 11 response.

13) How long have you been working in the market space? Over forty years

14) What was your first job? Small start-up company; didn't know if they would be able to meet payroll.

15) What valuable lessons have you learned over your career? Learned that you cannot do it alone; you need mentors, friends, family.

16) What type of spiritual life do you have? Have an active spiritual life; teaches him how to treat people.

17) Do you attend or engage in any religious activities? Yes, attends church on a regular basis.

18) What role has emotional intelligence played in your career progression? Has played more of a role as he has aged; he has learned from his experience; learned the importance of diversity of thought.

19) What are some unwritten rules or norms that you learned from being in a white-collar environment? Command and control is not the white-collar norm.

20) Did your parents or grandparents work in a white-collar setting? Yes or No? No

21) Did your parents or grandparents teach you how to navigate a white-collar working environment? No, they didn't know; grew up in rural Mississippi.

22) What did your parents or grandparents teach you about working in a white-collar environment? Values, Mom taught him to know that he could do whatever he wanted to do; just put your head into it.

23) How did you learn about these unwritten rules and norms (observation, mentors, mistakes)? All of the above

24) Currently, how many individuals do you mentor? Three to four people

25) How often do you listen or read about successful individuals? Daily; has a daily newsfeed

26) What role has self-talk played in your career success? Good/bad; it helps to pull him up; however, he can be his worst enemy as well.

27) How do you motivate yourself each day? Plan for the future; take care of his family.

28) What are some of your hobbies? Swim, read, crossword puzzles, brain games, pickle ball

29) Do you believe in the PIE model for career success? Yes, you need exposure to get the opportunities.

30) How often do you exercise? Four to five times per week

31) How much time do you take off each year to recharge your batteries? Four weeks of vacation

32) May I use your name in the book? (keep confidential) NA

33) Whom would you recommend that I interview for this book? NA

Blue- to White-Collar Thinking Interview (33 questions)
Send to Reginald Ramsey, PhD, MBA @ HRTC1906@gmail.com
Name: Black/Male/Manager
Response Date: September 20, 2017

1) What is your official job title? Associate vice chancellor for academic support, counseling, and bar preparation

2) How long have you been in your current role? Two months (however, position also serves as an associate professor of law, three years)

3) What attributes or skills helped you to reach your current career level? Education level, communication skills (written and oral), acquisition of knowledge and information, and interpersonal interactive skills

4) What does your typical day entail? Please, elaborate as much as possible.
Teaching law classes, managing staff of three professionals, interacting with students and administrators, discussing and implementing policies, and reviewing/researching various laws and concepts

5) How many hours do you work per week? Fifty to sixty hours per week

6) What advice would you give to someone who wants to be in your position someday? Be dedicated to your career, invest in it, and work hard to see the fruits of your labor, but remember that failure to attend to your personal life may have negative consequences away from the profession.

7) What has been the role of mentors or coaches in your career advancement? Very important in providing insight into the appropriateness of certain responses to events that take place in the work environment and providing historical context to events that may predate my time with the employer.

8) How many mentors do you have or have you had over your career? Approximately eight to ten

9) How often do you speak or communicate with your mentor/s? Weekly

10) How do you balance your work and life? Unfortunately, I am a workaholic, and it harmed the development of my personal life. If I could do it all over again, I would wait to start a family until my career had taken root.

11) How often do you set goals? Daily

12) What type of goals do you set? Yearly? Monthly? Et cetera? Short-term and long-term. Short-term goals could be for the day, week, or month depending on the situation.

13) How long have you been working in the market space? Twenty years (I assume that market space is used to define a professional position.)

14) What was your first job? Civil rights investigator in the federal government

15) What valuable lessons have you learned over your career? To treat everyone—even those who mistreat you—with respect, make certain to learn from every experience irrespective of whether you are the central character in the event, and always be the most informed person in the room (and if you are not, then find out how to become the most informed person in the room).

16) What type of spiritual life do you have? Active. I need the serenity provided by my spiritual life.

17) Do you attend or engage in any religious activities? Faithfully, on a weekly basis, and I pray multiple times during the day.

18) What role has emotional intelligence played in your career progression? I believe that I have a high emotional quotient (EQ), and I believe it has helped me as much as my intellect in advancing in my career.

19) What are some unwritten rules or norms that you learned from being in a white-collar environment?

    1. One should always be true to oneself because in tough times, the "real" you will be revealed, and your colleagues should be able to depend on you being you all of the time.

    2. Keep a positive outlook on life (both inside and outside of the office).

    3. Treat people fairly—with no exceptions.

    4. Avoid office gossip and mess.

20) Did your parents or grandparents work in a white-collar setting? Yes or No? My mother started in a white-collar job when I was in elementary school. All other family members worked in the blue-collar labor market.

21) Did your parents or grandparents teach you how to navigate a white-collar working environment? No, I learned to navigate this process without the benefit of a familial influence.

22) What did your parents or grandparents teach you about working in a white-collar environment? Indirectly, my parents instilled within me a good moral and spiritual base, and that has served as a wonderful foundation for my professional pursuits.

23) How did you learn about these unwritten rules and norms (observation, mentors, mistakes)? Life experience

24) Currently, how many individuals do you mentor? Four

25) How often do you listen or read about successful individuals? Probably twice a year.

26) What role has self-talk played in your career success? I talk to myself constantly, and occasionally I do answer back!

27) How do you motivate yourself each day? I pray that God will allow me to get out of His way as He delivers His promises to me.

28) What are some of your hobbies? Watching football and cookouts

29) Do you believe in the PIE model for career success? I had not previously heard of the model until seeing the question. I looked it up, and I do not think that my career behavior has been fully in accordance with the model. I focus on making certain my performance is top notch. My image is formed by how I present myself through my work and behavior. However, I have never worried about "protecting" or "projecting" my image to others. Additionally, I have never really sought exposure for my work. Instead, the quality of my work has resulted in me gaining exposure; however, such exposure was never contemplated prior to doing the work—it was simply a by-product of the production in my performance.

30) How often do you exercise? Daily, but that is new (last two years)

31) How much time do you take off each year to recharge your batteries? A couple of weeks for "scheduled" recharging, but I take breaks periodically when I can afford to steal a day or half of a day.

32) May I use your name in the book? (keep confidential) Yes

33) Whom would you recommend that I interview for this book? NA

Blue- to White-Collar Thinking Interview (33 questions)
Send to Reginald Ramsey, PhD, MBA @ HRTC1906@gmail.com
Name: White/Male/Professional
Response Date: 10/3/2017

1) What is your official job title? IT architect
2) How long have you been in your current role? 2005
3) What attributes or skills helped you to reach your current career level? Verbal skills; abilities to talk, listen; optimism
4) What does your typical day entail? Please, elaborate as much as possible. Consulting with management and talking to clients
5) How many hours do you work per week? Fifty to sixty hours a week
6) What advice would you give to someone who wants to be in your position someday? Keep current with technology; keep an open mind; key success urgency.
7) What has been the role of mentors or coaches in your career advancement? Encourage and guide, set their ideas, felt good and respected.
8) How many mentors do you have or have you had over your career? Six
9) How often do you speak or communicate with your mentor/s? Still interactive, monthly
10) How do you balance your work and life? Workaholic, poorly
11) How often do you set goals? Yearly, two to five years, self's and clients' goals
12) What type of goals do you set? Yearly? Monthly? Et cetera? Yearly
13) How long have you been working in the market space? Thirty-seven years
14) What was your first job? Information technology services

15) What valuable lessons have you learned over your career? Continuously renew yourself, technology perspective, people interactions.

16) What type of spiritual life do you have? Have spiritual/Christian beliefs and values

17) Do you attend or engage in any religious activities? Yes

18) What role has emotional intelligence played in your career progression? Learned to articulate his thoughts from his mentor (Bob Gibson)

19) What are some unwritten rules or norms that you learned from being in a white-collar environment? Speaking up for yourself. Competitive rules must be followed.

20) Did your parents or grandparents work in a white-collar setting? Yes or No? Yes

21) Did your parents or grandparents teach you how to navigate a white-collar working environment? Both were teachers, professors, no taught decorum, role models.

22) What did your parents or grandparents teach you about working in a white-collar environment? Hard work

23) How did you learn about these unwritten rules and norms (observation, mentors, mistakes)? All of the above

24) Currently, how many individuals do you mentor? Six or so

25) How often do you listen or read about successful individuals? Colin Powell, every time he went to a conference

26) What role has self-talk played in your career success? Fair amount

27) How do you motivate yourself each day? Habit; set the habit; don't have to do it all; just have to start … Starting is the hardest part.

28) What are some of your hobbies? Political junkie, notes to Congress, horseback riding

29) Do you believe in the PIE model for career success? Executive level agree, personal career

30) How often do you exercise? Three times per week

31) How much time do you take off each year to recharge your batteries? One to two weeks

32) May I use your name in the book? (keep confidential)

33) Whom would you recommend that I interview for this book?

Blue- to White-Collar Thinking Interview (33 questions)

Send to Reginald Ramsey, PhD, MBA @ HRTC1906@gmail.com

Name:__Black/Female/Professional_____

Response Date: ____12/3/2017_____

1) What is your official job title? Assistant project manager

2) How long have you been in your current role? Two years

3) What attributes or skills helped you to reach your current career level? Typing, accounting degree, being an excellent #2, having the gift of execution, and being a natural-born planner

4) What does your typical day entail? Please, elaborate as much as possible. Negotiating with stakeholders and trying to get a consensus and buy-in from all on the way forward on projects.

5) How many hours do you work per week? 37.5

6) What advice would you give to someone who wants to be in your position someday? They need to take good notes and be able to not take sides, listen to all points of view, and then make a decision.

7) What has been the role of mentors or coaches in your career advancement? I have never had an official mentor or coach. I have had advocates who have pushed me forward or have forced the hand of others to give me opportunities.

8) How many mentors do you have or have you had over your career? None

9) How often do you speak or communicate with your mentor/s? NA

10) How do you balance your work and life? I turn off my work phone after 6:00 p.m. and turn it back on at 7:00 a.m. on weekdays, and I turn my telephone off on weekends.

11) How often do you set goals? I only set personal goals now. I no longer set career goals. *We* do this twice a year, on our anniversary and New Year's Day.

12) What type of goals do you set? Yearly? Monthly? Et cetera? See #11.

13) How long have you been working in the market space? I have been in the project management industry for over twenty years.

14) What was your first job? Well, the first out of college was associate manager in finance, but my first job was a summer job through the SYEP program when I was a teenager as a summer school teacher's assistant.

15) What valuable lessons have you learned over your career? Producing and getting results matters most. Being a person of your word goes a long way. Your career will also go far and gain the respect of your management and peers if you don't make excuses when you mess up. Own it, and move forward.

16) What type of spiritual life do you have? A good one. I wouldn't be able to make it through the day without God. I pray daily and talk with God all day. My prayers include praying for my team at work and revealing to me what I need to know.

17) Do you attend or engage in any religious activities? Yes, I go to church weekly. I participate on the church's growth groups when I can. I try to stay engaged.

18) What role has emotional intelligence played in your career progression? No, I try not to be emotional at work.

19) What are some unwritten rules or norms that you learned from being in a white-collar environment? Women should not talk in a high shrill voice and too fast. We should not dress too sexy. It isn't respected. As a black person, I do need to work harder to get the same pay as my white peers.

20) Did your parents or grandparents work in a white-collar setting? Yes or No? Yes, my dad was computer scientist, and my mom was schoolteacher.

21) Did your parents or grandparents teach you how to navigate a white-collar working environment? No

22) What did your parents or grandparents teach you about working in a white-collar environment? Nothing really. They just said you cannot trust the white man, and I couldn't wear my hair naturally.

23) How did you learn about these unwritten rules and norms (observation, mentors, mistakes)? Mistakes, observation.

24) Currently, how many individuals do you mentor? None

25) How often do you listen or read about successful individuals? Once a year, I will pick up a book on someone.

26) What role has self-talk played in your career success? Lots. My motto is fake it till you make it, and live by Colossians 3:23.

27) How do you motivate yourself each day? Every morning in the car on the way to work, and I have Colossians 3:23 posted in my office so I can see it from my desk. I also have pictures up of times that made me happy. It reminds me of why I work.

28) What are some of your hobbies? Traveling, going to the SPA

29) Do you believe in the PIE model for career success? I do not know anything about PIE.

30) How often do you exercise? Four to five days a week

31) How much time do you take off each year to recharge your batteries? Three to four weeks

32) May I use your name in the book? (keep confidential)

33) Whom would you recommend that I interview for this book?

CHAPTER 7

SURVEY RESULTS VI

Blue- to White-Collar Thinking Interview (33 questions)
Send to Reginald Ramsey, PhD, MBA @ HRTC1906@gmail.com
Name: Black/Female/Professional
Response Date: 9/27/2017 and 10/4/2017

1) What is your official job title? Senior health care IT consultant
2) How long have you been in your current role? Six years
3) What attributes or skills helped you to reach your current career level? Customer service skills, personality, listening, provide data
4) What does your typical day entail? Please, elaborate as much as possible. Working with tickets, SQL code, Microsoft SQL database; validate data
5) How many hours do you work per week? Forty
6) What advice would you give to someone who wants to be in your position someday? Education in computer technology, shadow someone.
7) What has been the role of mentors or coaches in your career advancement? Really haven't taken advantage of this, had one or two.
8) How many mentors do you have or have you had over your career? Five
9) How often do you speak or communicate with your mentor/s? Two to three times a year
10) How do you balance your work and life? Plan ahead, have outside volunteering activities.
11) How often do you set goals? Four to five times, daily goals

12) What type of goals do you set? Yearly? Monthly? Et cetera? Weekly, monthly, yearly

13) How long have you been working in the market space? Twenty-eight years

14) What was your first job? Senior programmer

15) What valuable lessons have you learned over your career? Try to be a listener; pay attention around you; listen mode.

16) What type of spiritual life do you have? Prayerful, thank God, does consist with daily Bible plan

17) Do you attend or engage in any religious activities? Attend church, Bible class.

18) What role has emotional intelligence played in your career progression? Learned IT customer, not to work personal services, keep emotions out, keep emotions in check, stay focused, and get the job done.

19) What are some unwritten rules or norms that you learned from being in a white-collar environment? Manager in title may not be calling the shots

20) Did your parents or grandparents work in a white-collar setting? Yes or No? Mom (RN-blue collar, steel mind)

21) Did your parents or grandparents teach you how to navigate a white-collar working environment? Mom—told her to know her rights, what employee manual says

22) What did your parents or grandparents teach you about working in a white-collar environment? Get a copy, union mentality, know the rules

23) How did you learn about these unwritten rules and norms (observation, mentors, mistakes)? All of the above

24) Currently, how many individuals do you mentor? Two young ladies in HR field

25) How often do you listen or read about successful individuals? A lot, monthly

26) What role has self-talk played in your career success? Role: help to navigate in the workplace

27) How do you motivate yourself each day? Think about the final end goal.

28) What are some of your hobbies? Movies, plays, concerts, theater, reading, politics

29) Do you believe in the PIE model for career success? I agree, relationship

30) How often do you exercise? Not enough

31) How much time do you take off each year to recharge your batteries? A lot in the past two weeks

32) May I use your name in the book? (keep confidential) NA

33) Whom would you recommend that I interview for this book? She has a friend; she will touch base with them first.

Blue- to White-Collar Thinking Interview (33 questions)
Send to Reginald Ramsey, PhD, MBA @ HRTC1906@gmail.com
Name: Female, Black, Professional
Response Date: 10/16/17

1) What is your official job title? Adjunct professor in business administration programs

2) How long have you been in your current role? Four years

3) What attributes or skills helped you to reach your current career level? The skills that helped me reach my current career level are being able to maintain an expertise in the field of business and being sensitive to, and understanding of, the diverse academic, socioeconomic, cultural, disability, and ethnic backgrounds of college students.

4) What does your typical day entail? Please, elaborate as much as possible.
Monday–Friday:
7:00 a.m.–9:00 a.m. office, emails, class prep, et cetera …
Mon., Tues., Thurs., Fri., 9:00a.m.–11:00 a.m. teach class
11:00 a.m. lunch
Wed., 10:00 a.m.–11:00 a.m. departmental meeting
11:00 a.m.–2:00 p.m. office hours
Fri. 1:00 p.m. work with research group
Fri. 2:00 p.m. meet with departmental manager every other Friday
2:00 p.m.–4:00 p.m. list of the following happens …

✓ Read and clear yet more email
✓ Deal with tasks induced by email
✓ Write papers for journal interest
✓ Prepare class
✓ Organize research group events
✓ Perform developmental department needs

✓ Perform university service
✓ Perform any community service

5) How many hours do you work per week? Between forty and fifty hours per week

6) What advice would you give to someone who wants to be in your position someday? Aim to be great in teaching, research, impacting others, service, and outreach for the community.

7) What has been the role of mentors or coaches in your career advancement? The role of my mentors helped by being committed, a good listener, set goals for my career path, and being a role model by sharing their experiences.

8) How many mentors do you have or have you had over your career? Two

9) How often do you speak or communicate with your mentor/s? Monthly

10) How do you balance your work and life? I do this by prioritizing. This helps in deciding what to keep and what to discard. For example, I realize that I might not be able to volunteer with three nonprofit organizations. I select the most meaningful one, focus on it, and stop scattering my attention among all three.

11) How often do you set goals? I set goals weekly, monthly, and yearly.

12) What type of goals do you set? Yearly? Monthly? Et cetera? I set goals that are specific, measureable, achievable, results-focused, and time bound. I make sure that the goals are written and are defined of what needs to be done.

13) How long have you been working in the market space? Four years

14) What was your first job? Working in the kitchen of a nursing facility.

15) What valuable lessons have you learned over your career? I have learned to have patience, embrace challenges, not to underestimate

the value of my skills, and to always keep an open mind because learning never stops.

16) What type of spiritual life do you have? I do practice having a sense of peace and purpose with my Christian beliefs.

17) Do you attend or engage in any religious activities? Yes

18) What role has emotional intelligence played in your career progression? The role in my EI is understanding the characteristic of self-awareness. I do not let my feelings rule me. I am confident and trust myself to not allow my emotions to get out of control, especially under stress.

19) What are some unwritten rules or norms that you learned from being in a white-collar environment? Many times, I had to evaluate if an organizational culture will put me in the position for my success. I have learned the importance of accessing the culture and determining if it aligns with my values.

20) Did your parents or grandparents work in a white-collar setting? Yes or No? No, they retired as blue-collar workers.

21) Did your parents or grandparents teach you how to navigate a white-collar working environment? No, my older brother did, after he graduated from medical school.

22) What did your parents or grandparents teach you about working in a white-collar environment? My parents taught me about getting an education and to aim for whatever I wanted to do in life. They created a path for us to be successful, regardless of whether we worked in a blue- or white-collar environment.

23) How did you learn about these unwritten rules and norms (observation, mentors, mistakes)? Observation

24) Currently, how many individuals do you mentor? Three

25) How often do you listen or read about successful individuals? Once a day

26) What role has self-talk played in your career success? If I understand this question, this is the role of talking to yourself. Most times I cheer myself on, focus on positive aspects of a situation, and allow myself to feel good about what I have done.

27) How do you motivate yourself each day? I reduce daily distractions and get motivated from people in my life. I play music that gives me energy. I am optimistic, and if setbacks occur, I have taken the opportunity to learn from them and improve.

28) What are some of your hobbies? I enjoy reading, movies, traveling, paintings, and visiting art galleries.

29) Do you believe in the PIE model for career success? Yes, I do agree with the PIE model for career success—especially with image, because this is about reputation, including how others perceive me. People often form an opinion of me before ever meeting me. This can result from the following: a) the results, I have historically delivered; b) the credibility I have established within the company (Am I ethical, fair, or trustworthy?); c) my work style (collaborative or confrontational, personally engaging?); and d) my operational savviness. I value my work environment and understand that behaviors shape my image.

30) How often do you exercise? Only two times a week.

31) How much time do you take off each year to recharge your batteries? I take off during the summer months, especially in the month of July to enjoy myself and family events.

32) May I use your name in the book? Sure (keep confidential)

33) Whom would you recommend that I interview for this book? Dr. Parks and Dr. Riley

Blue- to White-Collar Thinking Interview (33 questions)
Send to Reginald Ramsey, PhD, MBA @ HRTC1906@gmail.com
Name: Black/Female/Professional
Response Date: September 10, 2017

1) What is your official job title? Associate professor of legal analysis and writing

2) How long have you been in your current role? Ten years

3) What attributes or skills helped you to reach your current career level? Excellent public speaking skills, excellent research and writing skills, personal commitment to professionalism and ethics.

4) What does your typical day entail? Please, elaborate as much as possible. On days that I have classes, I usually spend at least two to three hours before each class preparing for class by reading briefing cases, preparing lecture materials, preparing exercises and assignments. During office hours, I usually meet with students. I meet with students enrolled in my classes to discuss how they are progressing and areas of improvement needed. I also serve as an advisor to some students who are writing law review articles. I also meet with these students regularly to discuss ideas for their articles and to assist them with the writing process. On days that I do not have classes, I try to spend at least three to four hours researching and/or writing. I also spend several hours per day grading various assignments for my legal analysis and writing students (students are usually assigned at least one essay per week that I grade and provide detailed feedback on). I also serve on a number of committees at work, and I am a CASA advocate; thus, at least eight to ten hours per week are spent either in meetings, in training, or involved in CASA-related activities.

5) How many hours do you work per week? I try not to work more than forty-five to fifty hours; however, I often work about fifty-five to sixty hours per week.

6) What advice would you give to someone who wants to be in your position someday? To become a professor, a person needs high academic performance and considerable extracurricular and community involvement (law review, moot court, student government association, et cetera).

7) What has been the role of mentors or coaches in your career advancement? While I have had a couple of mentors, I think mentor involvement in my career development and advancement has been minimal. I also think that had I done a better job of these mentoring opportunities, I'd be further in my career. However, I realized that personal fulfillment (enjoying life) is more important to me than reaching the "top" of my organization.

8) How many mentors do you have or have you had over your career? Two

9) How often do you speak or communicate with your mentor/s? Rarely. Instead, I have a strong network of colleagues and similarly situated individuals with whom I discuss my career and theirs. We help one another.

10) How do you balance your work and life? I devote at least ten to fifteen hours per week to myself for exercise, meditation, leisure, and/or socializing. I also try to take at least two personal trips per year.

11) How often do you set goals? Not as often as I used to, not as often as I should. Too many short-term deadlines seem to be clouding my long-term planning these days. Also, my focus has shifted to having more leisure time and less work in recent months.

12) What type of goals do you set? Yearly? Monthly? Et cetera? Now I'm in short-term mode, so, most of my goals are really weekly and monthly "to do" lists. I do set one-year, five-year, and ten-year goals.

13) How long have you been working in the market space? I have been an attorney for twenty-two years. I started my first job while in high school (in 1987).

14) What was your first job? My first job ever was as a clerical assistant in my uncle's solo law practice. My first career-related job was while I was in law school as a law clerk at the Louisiana Department of Environmental Quality. My first job as a lawyer was as an associate at a large law firm in New Orleans (McGlinchey Stafford).

15) What valuable lessons have you learned over your career? I have learned so many lessons. However, I think the most important lessons I have learned are to stay true to who I am and my core values of strong work ethic and always being ethical and professional. I have seen many others cut corners and compromise their values. While in the short-term they may have had some success, in the long-term, they have paid high prices (e.g., loss of respect from clients, colleagues, and others and/or license and career in jeopardy).

16) What type of spiritual life do you have? I spend time each morning meditating. I read a daily devotional and related Bible passages. I also attend church about once per month.

17) Do you attend or engage in any religious activities? I attend church about once per month.

18) What role has emotional intelligence played in your career progression? I'm not sure what "emotional intelligence" involves. However, I am generally able to keep emotion out of my career and remain objective in decision-making. I have had occasions where emotions (particularly with respect to people who have no work ethic and/or no respect for others) clouded my judgment. Those situations have taught me that personal feelings and emotions should be at a minimum (if at all) in the workplace.

19) What are some unwritten rules or norms that you learned from being in a white-collar environment?

20) Did your parents or grandparents work in a white-collar setting? Yes or No? No. None did.

21) Did your parents or grandparents teach you how to navigate a white-collar working environment? No. Absolutely *not*.

22) What did your parents or grandparents teach you about working in a white-collar environment? None of them worked in a white-collar environment, so I doubt any of the lessons taught to me were geared toward that environment. However, they did teach me certain life lessons that are important in any environment, such as respecting oneself and others, being a person of my word, and having a strong spiritual life.

23) How did you learn about these unwritten rules and norms (observation, mentors, mistakes)? I have learned a lot by observing the behavior and mistakes of others. I have also received invaluable advice and training from former supervisors, colleagues, and mentors. Unfortunately, much of my education has come from my own mistakes, especially with respect to the politics and social interactions involved.

24) Currently, how many individuals do you mentor? Just because of my role at the Southern University Law Center as a professor (and formerly as a career development professional), I mentor several people at any given point in time. Usually, I have a very close mentoring relationship with between five and ten people.

25) How often do you listen or read about successful individuals? Not often. I don't really have a lot of "free" time these days because I'm in my research and writing cycle. However, I tried to read at least one or two nonfiction books per year.

26) What role has self-talk played in your career success? Early in my educational experience, I learned about positive reinforcement

and self-fulfilling prophesies. Thus, I have always had several daily mantras that motivate me and keep me focused and positive.

27) How do you motivate yourself each day? I start my day with a devotional reading and a positive affirmation. I also recite daily mantras to myself in the mirror as I get dressed for the day.

28) What are some of your hobbies? I exercise a lot. I am currently training for a one-quarter marathon. I enjoy leisure reading. I also enjoy traveling. I also try to get out of the house to see a live band or go dancing or some similar activity at least once a month.

29) Do you believe in the PIE model for career success? I am not familiar with this success model.

30) How often do you exercise? At least one-hour per day five days per week.

31) How much time do you take off each year to recharge your batteries? I usually take one to two weeks off in summer and one to two weeks off in December/January.

32) May I use your name in the book? (keep confidential) Yes

33) Whom would you recommend that I interview for this book?

Blue- to White-Collar Thinking Interview (33 questions)
Send to Reginald Ramsey, PhD, MBA @ HRTC1906@gmail.com
Name: Black/Male/Executive
Response Date: 9/25/2017

1) What is your official job title? President, CEO

2) How long have you been in your current role? Seventeen years

3) What attributes or skills helped you to reach your current career level? Emotional intelligence, boldness, conviction, finding your own voice

4) What does your typical day entail? Please, elaborate as much as possible. Presentations, research clients, and complying

5) How many hours do you work per week? Sixty hours per week

6) What advice would you give to someone who wants to be in your position someday? Convince; have a solution; present to the world.

7) What has been the role of mentors or coaches in your career advancement? Beneficial, virtual mentor

8) How many mentors do you have or have you had over your career? Five to six, various points in his life

9) How often do you speak or communicate with your mentor/s? Weekly

10) How do you balance your work and life? Poor example, tried to make the most of time with his wife.

11) How often do you set goals? Annually, calibrate quarterly, and weekly deliverable

12) What type of goals do you set? Yearly? Monthly? Et cetera? Week delivering

13) How long have you been working in the market space? Thirty-four years

14) What was your first job? Instructor, business college, math, English, cognitive science

15) What valuable lessons have you learned over your career? Don't underestimate impact or value.

16) What type of spiritual life do you have? Integral to his identity; given gifts

17) Do you attend or engage in any religious activities? Yes

18) What role has emotional intelligence played in your career progression? Very important perspective, feeling, thinking

19) What are some unwritten rules or norms that you learned from being in a white-collar environment? Better to build allies than to build friends.

20) Did your parents or grandparents work in a white-collar setting? Yes or No? Mom was a nurse, RN, respected.

21) Did your parents or grandparents teach you how to navigate a white-collar working environment? No, nothing formal, expectant

22) What did your parents or grandparents teach you about working in a white-collar environment? Have to be better than good; being average will not cut it.

23) How did you learn about these unwritten rules and norms (observation, mentors, mistakes)? All of the above

24) Currently, how many individuals do you mentor? Relationship five to six individuals, regular conversations

25) How often do you listen or read about successful individuals? Often loved to read biographies, case studies

26) What role has self-talk played in your career success? Very important

27) How do you motivate yourself each day? Goal; work to accomplish; help people

28) What are some of your hobbies? Unknown

29) Do you believe in the PIE model for career success? Yes, absolutely

30) How often do you exercise? Not enough

31) How much time do you take off each year to recharge your batteries? Two to three days periodically
32) May I use your name in the book? (keep confidential)
33) Whom would you recommend that I interview for this book?

Blue- to White-Collar Thinking Interview (33 questions)
Send to Reginald Ramsey, PhD, MBA @ HRTC1906@gmail.com
Name: Black/Male/Executive
Response Date: 10/3/2017

1) What is your official job title? Superintendent

2) How long have you been in your current role? Three years

3) What attributes or skills helped you to reach your current career level? Education, PhD, and two master's degrees, networking with mentors.

4) What does your typical day entail? Please, elaborate as much as possible. Meetings, interacting with different groups, meeting with lawmakers, works on different boards.

5) How many hours do you work per week? Works seventy hours a week

6) What advice would you give to someone who wants to be in your position someday? Get the best education; understand the value of mentors.

7) What has been the role of mentors or coaches in your career advancement? Mentors provide advice, data, creating visions

8) How many mentors do you have or have you had over your career? One hundred mentors, since elementary school

9) How often do you speak or communicate with your mentor/s? Stay in contact on a monthly basis, by calls and meeting for coffee sessions.

10) How do you balance your work and life? Not well, work/success/money

11) How often do you set goals? Daily goals, every six months, one year

12) What type of goals do you set? Yearly? Monthly? Et cetera? Daily, yearly

13) How long have you been working in the market space? Fifty-three years

14) What was your first job? First black teacher in Portage, Michigan

15) What valuable lessons have you learned over your career? Value of hard work, focus, sound settings

16) What type of spiritual life do you have? Strong, believes in God.

17) Do you attend or engage in any religious activities? Attends Sunday school at different churches; attends Bible school.

18) What role has emotional intelligence played in your career progression? A tremendous role, high EQ started with his grandparents and his parents.

19) What are some unwritten rules or norms that you learned from being in a white-collar environment? Listen to what is not being said. (We have two ears and one mouth.)

20) Did your parents or grandparents work in a white-collar setting? Yes or No? No

21) Did your parents or grandparents teach you how to navigate a white-collar working environment? Thought, business, blue collar

22) What did your parents or grandparents teach you about working in a white-collar environment? Work hard, ten times better, have confidence.

23) How did you learn about these unwritten rules and norms (observation, mentors, mistakes)? All of the above

24) Currently, how many individuals do you mentor? More than twenty supervisors

25) How often do you listen or read about successful individuals? Daily, love to read biographies.

26) What role has self-talk played in your career success? Talks a lot to himself.

27) How do you motivate yourself each day? Wake up motivated, gospels, work, half full, pray, optimistic

28) What are some of your hobbies? Hunting, fishing, golf, reading

29) According to Harvey Coleman, it takes performance, image, and exposure (PIE) to succeed in the white-collar area, do you believe in the PIE model for career success? Yes

30) How often do you exercise? Two times per week

31) How much time do you take off each year to recharge your batteries? Two times a week

32) May I use your name in the book? (keep confidential) NA

33) Whom would you recommend that I interview for this book? NA

CHAPTER 8

BLUE- VERSUS WHITE-COLLAR THINKING

Warning/Note: This list is not exhaustive. These are only the observations of the author. Please review and reflect on the list. Again, these are only the observations and views of the author.

Patterns of Blue-Collar versus White-Collar Individuals

Blue Collar	White Collar
1) Paid by the hour	Paid by salary (stocks / stock options)
2) Brown-nosing	Networking for success
3) Prefer to work alone, "I"	Must work in global teams, "we"
4) Work is performance/task based	Work is performance/image/exposure
5) Feedback is task-oriented	Feedback is goals-oriented
6) Limited to no formal education/training	Plenty of formal education/training
7) Limited to no credentials to advance	Multiple credentials to advance
8) Reads less than one book per year	Reading on a regular basis
9) Do not believe in mentoring to grow	Mentoring is the key to their growth
10) Emotional intelligence (EI) is not a priority	Works to improve emotional intelligence (EI)
11) Saves money	Invests and saves money

12) Renting is okay; home ownership is a goal	Home ownership is a priority
13) No sponsorship at work	Have sponsor/s to open doors at work
14) Many are not college educated	Many are college educated
15) Family oriented	Family oriented
16) Limited study habits	Studying various topics and subjects
17) Strong faith beliefs	Strong faith beliefs
18) Works forty hours per week	Works greater than fifty hours per week
19) Goals are limited, not written	Goals are big, written down, SMART
20) Limited to no knowledge of unwritten rules / social norms in white-collar setting	Learn unwritten rules / social norms from mentors, coaches, others
21) Do not ask for help	Willing to ask for help

Blue Collar Thinking

- Use terms and phrases like "I," "I can do it myself," "I don't like to work in teams," "The team is slowing me down"
- Was told at home to "work hard to achieve success in life"
- Membership includes unions and trade unions
- Don't believe in the power of career networking, is considered a weakness
- Many believe in an adversarial role with their supervisor/manager
- Many believe that a high school diploma / GED is enough to succeed in life
- Many believe in renting / leasing a home / car / material items
- Many believe that a good time involves beer and hard beverages

- Don't believe in attending lecture series to expand knowledge
- Rarely belong to organizations such as public speaking or scholarly organizations
- Watch sports like football, baseball, basketball, and automobile racing (common to white-collar individuals as well)
- Many will encourage their kids to get trades and work with their hands
- Prefer to do things like "their parents and/or grandparents"
- Many will maintain a "limited" to no household budget
- Typically do not teach kids how to budget and invest their money wisely
- Believe in instant gratification
- Have an "excuse for everything" attitude (it's always someone's fault instead of theirs)
- Don't always maintain cool and calm demeanor under adverse circumstances
- Don't like to received feedback on how their behavior is affecting others
- The skill of active listening is not a strong trait
- Listen to sports and talk radio programs
- Form their opinions based on a radio host/s
- Form their opinions based on a TV host/s
- Do not have a passport
- Have not traveled outside of their country of origin
- Prefer to save money in a safe fashion
- Believe in the lottery as their ticket out of poverty
- Believe one big break will free them (i.e., sports basketball, baseball, football)
- Attend public schools
- Focused on material possessions (cars, houses, jewelry, and so on)

- Do not believe in the power of reading to develop one's life (read less than one book per year)
- Read plenty of gossip newspapers
- Love to learn about athletes, superstars, and so on
- Lean toward the Democratic Party platform values
- Relish the opportunity to engage in a toxic argument over a trivial matter (i.e., shoes, clothes, word choices, and so on)
- Tend to be ill-read and not able to converse on a variety subjects/topics
- When dealt a setback (i.e., job loss), don't confide in friends but try to solve it by themselves

White-Collar Thinking

- Use terms and phrases like "team" and "we can do it"
- Was told at home to work in teams to achieve success in life
- Belong to fraternities, sororities, social club organizations
- Believe in the power of career networking to become successful
- Believe in a strong working relationship with their supervisor/boss
- Believe in obtaining transferrable skills
- Believe in the power of a college degree from an accredited university/college
- Believe a good time is with friends and family
- Believe in home ownership
- Believe in stocks/bonds ownership
- Believe in the power of their business
- Participate in lecture series to expand knowledge of a variety of subjects
- Belong to global organizations such as Toastmasters and other scholarly organizations
- Play sports like tennis, golf, and skiing

- Watch sports like tennis, golf, and swimming
- Encourage kids to become doctors, lawyers, engineers, and businesspeople
- Encourage kids to obtain advanced degrees and work using their minds
- Embrace and encourage new ideas
- Maintain a robust household budget
- Teach kids how to budget and invest wisely
- Believe very strongly in delayed gratification
- Have a "no excuses, just results" attitude and mentality
- Embrace feedback on how their behavior is impacting others (360-degree feedback, one-on-one feedback, and so on)
- Some may love to listen to understand
- Some may listen to motivational speakers
- Listen to both conservative and progressive views via radio/TV/internet
- Form their opinions based on factual information
- Time watching TV is kept to a minimum (prefers to read and/or learn a different language)
- Have a passport
- Have traveled out of the country of origin
- Prefer to save money in creative ways (stocks, bonds, real estate, and so on)
- Believe in the power of ownership so they can employ others (basketball, baseball, football players)
- Believe in the power of planning and setting goals to achieve their success
- Believe in making their breaks
- Attend public, private, and exclusive schools
- Focus on developing themselves through books, seminars, courses, travel, and so on

- Believe in the power of reading to develop one's life (read more than one book per year)
- Subscribe to various newspapers (*New York Times, Wall Street Journal, Washington Post, LA Times,* and so on)
- Have a great passion for learning new things
- Lean toward the Independent to Republican Party platform and/ or values
- Love to acquaint with like-minded and success-oriented individuals
- Relish the opportunity to engage in a heated discussion over big ideas that impact a company, community, family, global society
- Tend to be well-read and able to discuss various topics
- When dealt a major setback (i.e., job loss), confide in close friends or relatives, have a team of people working to help them[1]

Blue to White Summary

With all of these differences between blue and white thinking, is it possible for a blue-collar individual to change and become a white-collar-thinking person? My answer to this question is emphatically, *yes*. The blue-collar individual must be willing to accept candid and direct feedback and to change from the inside with the hope that the outside will manifest that change. I would love to tell you that the change process will be short, quick, and brief. However, that would not be truthful. The brutal fact of the matter is that the change process will take some time. We are talking five years or more. Real change is not a quick process.

Moreover, how is it possible to change oneself? The first step in fixing the problem is to recognize and acknowledge the problem. The second step is to figure out a way or create a plan to change your thought process. I would like to say it will be easy. However, it will not be. The journey

---

[1] "For Growing Ranks of the White-Collar Jobless, Support with a Touch of the Spur," *New York Times*, January 25, 2009.

will be filled with false starts and quick endings. It will be filled with disappointments and setbacks. However, you must persevere and persist because the rewards can be so fulfilling at so many levels. Among the rewards can be a better relationship with your family, friends, supervisors, and coworkers. You will be able to understand the corporate game and navigate the terrain much better. There is an art to the corporate game. There is an art to becoming the best you that you can be. You can become the man or woman that you want to be. It only takes a commitment to change. In addition, the process of change is an emotional event in one's life. Therefore, let's explore the subject of emotional intelligence.

Nontraditional College Students

Forbus, Newbold, and Mehta (2010) indicated that there are a growing number of nontraditional college students. They defined the nontraditional students as individuals who have not followed a continuous educational path into college. They typically are older than traditional college students (Evelyn, 2002). Nontraditional students tend to be more diverse than younger students in their expectations of the college or university. These students are motivated to attend college because of their experiences in life and their careers. Nontraditional students have to broaden their general outlook on education and life (Forbus, Newbold, and Mehta, 2011).

The size of the nontraditional student population has increased (Forbus et al., 2010). This student population is characterized as being over twenty-four-years-old, working full-time, and often having dependents or children to support. Many of the nontraditional students attend college on a part-time basis (Forbus et al., 2011). Bye, Pushkar, and Conway (2007) indicated that between 1996 and 2006, the number of nontraditional undergraduate college students increased at a rate of 30 percent to 50 percent.

Forbus et al. (2011) posited that over the last fifty years, US employment has gradually shifted from manufacturing blue-collar jobs to white-collar, service-related professions. With this job shift, more adults are becoming nontraditional students (Forbus et al., 2011).

Higher education has allowed the nontraditional student to prepare for a career change (Forbus et al., 2011). Morris, Brooks, and May (2003) indicated that nontraditional students have significantly more time and role tensions than traditional college students. The nontraditional students are more stressed and apprehensive (Morris et al., 2003).

Forbus, et al. (2011) indicated that nontraditional students are presented with stressful situations more often during their higher education journey because of work-related, social, and domestic situations. The nontraditional student has more time constraints and less involvement in the college campus life. He or she can be financially stressed, having to balance college tuition, rent, vehicle and transportation costs, and other life events (Forbus et. al., 2011). With the increase of nontraditional students attending college, there is a need to understand how this group is impacted by their current life situation and how they cope with the pressures of college life (Forbus et al., 2011). The construct of emotional intelligence may help to provide assistance to this student population throughout their college life and careers (Forbus et al., 2011).

College Students' Challenges

First-year college students' decision to matriculate and complete a college degree is an important one. There are a number of obstacles that are presented throughout the students' academic path. There is a convergence of disorientating dilemmas, such as layoffs, business closings, dwindling retirement accounts, declining job market, returning to school, and retirement itself. These economic factors are increasing the number of older adults looking for retraining at colleges (Peters, 2010). A college education can become the path for this population to be retrained and reengaged in civic and work activities (Zeiss, 2006). With a college education, one is able to attain more financial and personal freedom. Some college students are able to overcome their obstacles while others are not. The association between emotional intelligence and the first-year college students' decisions to complete their degrees will be examined and explored.

Colleges and universities are facing increased pressures from the recent economic downturn. Okpala, Hopson, and Okpala (2011) found that the current economic crisis has affected and will continue to impact colleges and universities in North Carolina and other states in the United States. These colleges and universities will be affected in the areas of funding, student support services, and student enrollment. Okpala et al. (2011) found that the effects of budget reductions in state funding are more profound in colleges and universities. Grubb (2001) also found that student support programs are vulnerable to budget reductions because of the abundance of part-time tutors and counselors. Okpala, Hopson, and Okpala's (2011) survey data showed that the national economic crisis resulted in severe cuts in student support services, especially in the area of counseling and advising. As one college official indicated,

> "I see an erosion of quality especially in basic education arena with the use of unqualified part-time faculty. Another one indicated that there is a need for counselors at my community college because students need to be properly advised in order to be successful, but we cannot hire due to the budget restriction" (Okpala, Hopson, and Okpala, 2011).

One overarching theme that emerged from the analysis was fear of further budget cuts and their implications for the quality of teaching and learning at local colleges (Okpala, Hopson, and Okpala, 2011).

Grubb, Badway, Bell, and Castellano (2000) stated that colleges are important in meeting the training demands of the subbaccalaureate sector of the workforce. Grubb (1999) emphasized that colleges are key to dealing with workforce shortages and job training. A good college education has been known to be the most cost-effective way to provide access for students to improve their life situation (Phelam, 2000).

Emotional intelligence is an important influencing variable in personal achievement, career success, leadership, and life satisfaction (Nelson and Low, 2003). Emotional intelligence determines how people exercise self-control, zeal, persistence, and the ability to motivate themselves (Goleman, 1995).

Peters (2010) asserted that economic factors (such as layoffs, business closings, dwindling retirement accounts, declining job market, returning to school, and retirement) are increasing the number of older adults looking for retraining through a college education. To accommodate this growing need, colleges need to know what draws this cohort to their campuses. The influence of the boomer generation (US citizens born between 1946 and 1964) to college is an emerging field where more information is needed. There is a growing need from the boomers for career classes (Peters, 2010). Yarrish and Law (2009) found that students are in need of an increased emotional intelligence development in all areas. They recommended their study on emotional intelligence and first-year students should be replicated comparing all students at colleges or universities in the United States.

A review of the literature reveals a limited number of studies have investigated the association between emotional intelligence and first-year college students' career intentions. This study investigated how emotional intelligence can affect first-year college students' career intentions. In addition, this study explored their motivation to continue with their education and graduate.

Hannah and Robinson (1990) indicated that many college students need assistance in navigating their college life. Many college graduates seek and need help with their career planning as well. From a global perspective, over 50 percent of college freshmen in the United States seek professional advice in choosing a career (Hannah and Robinson, 1990). In Korea, the number of students seeking career counseling regarding schoolwork and future career paths has sharply increased (Han, Yang, and Choi, 2001; Kim and Oh, 1991; Lee and Han, 1997). Lee (2005) indicated that the growing demand for career counseling among college students suggests that the preparation and decision-making stages involved in career decisions are becoming increasingly stressful and confusing.

The specific problem this research will address is students need to be more informed about the career decision process and ways of resolving psychological difficulties they may encounter during this process (Gati, Krausz, and Osipow, 1996). In addition, colleges need information to provide in-depth services to their students (Peters, 2010).

Purpose of the Study

The purpose of this study is to examine the association between emotional intelligence and first-year college students' intentions to complete their degrees. The independent variable will be emotional intelligence (EIS), and the dependent variable will be intentions of first-year college students (CCI). Yarrish and Law (2009) indicated that educators need to take seriously the responsibility of empowering the next generation of students with tools to assist them in their life's pursuits. According to National Public Radio (NPR), the graduation rates for first-year college students are very low. This research attempts to address the question of what motivates first-year college students to matriculate and complete their college degrees.

In today's competitive and global environment, it is imperative that first-year college students are able to make clear and sound decisions. For this research, the association between emotional intelligence and first-year college students' intentions to complete their college degrees was investigated. This study attempted to help in understanding if a significant association exists between emotional intelligence and first-year college students' intentions to complete their degrees.

CHAPTER 9

EMOTIONAL INTELLIGENCE

Global employers have long been calling for higher levels of personal and interpersonal skills among the college graduates they hire (Porter and McKibbin, 1988). Global companies are looking for creative means to grow and stay profitable. Gostick and Elton (2007) indicated that there is a need to develop and utilize every employee to his or her full potential, without losing the high-potential employees. Global companies are looking for innovative means to achieve this worthy goal. There are obstacles that may thwart this goal for some individuals. The importance of developing each employee regardless of his or her background, culture, national origin, ethnicity, and gender is vitally important to the success of any global corporation.

Goleman (1995) indicated that emotional intelligence might play a role in developing personal and interpersonal skills. Goleman (1995) defined emotional intelligence as the ability to recognize and understand emotions and the skill to use this awareness to manage oneself and one's associations with others. Emotional intelligence consists of five components: knowing one's emotions, managing emotions, motivating oneself, recognizing emotions in other people, and handling associations (Goleman, 1995).

Emotional intelligence has been investigated in several recent studies. Schumacher, Wheeler, and Carr (2009) studied the association between emotional intelligence and buyers' performance. They found that buyers' emotional intelligence is positively related to association performance, most significantly from the perspective of their key suppliers. Depape, Hakim-Larson, Voelker, Page, and Jackson (2006) researched the association of emotional intelligence and self-talk on Canadian university students. Self-talk has been discussed in the literature as a means of enhancing self-awareness and self-regulation, both of which are considered important in the construct of emotional intelligence. Depape et al. (2006) found significant positive relations between emotional intelligence and self-talk. Yarrish and Law (2009) explored the difference in emotional intelligence of first-year business students. Yarrish and Law (2009) found that students are in need of an increased emotional intelligence development in all areas. In addition, research by Shipley, Jackson, and Segrest (2010) posited the effects of emotional intelligence on age, work experience, and academic performance. Shipley et al. (2010) found that age was not positively correlated with emotional intelligence. However, work experience and academic performance were (Shipley et al., 2010).

Emotional intelligence, in laymen's terms, can be thought of as how one relates to and gets along with other people. In other words, it is how you build and maintain relations with other people. Some people are very good at making and maintaining friends. However, some people are not. In the white-collar business environment, it is important to be able to build and maintain friendships, especially with those in positions of power and authority.

Emotional Intelligence Defined

Research on emotional intelligence (EI) began as early as the 1930s with researchers Thorndike and Stein (1937) and Wechsler (1943). Wechsler (1958) defined intelligence as the global capacity of an individual or person to act purposefully, to think rationally, and to work harmoniously and congruently with his or her environment. Wechsler (1943) posited that total intelligence cannot be measured without some level of nonintellective factors being included. Gardner (1983) wrote about multiple intelligences and proposed that intrapersonal and interpersonal intelligence are as important as the type of intelligence typically measured by traditional intelligence (IQ) and related tests (Webb, 2009).

Salovey and Mayer (1990, 189) indicated that emotional intelligence included an "ability to monitor one's own and others' feelings and emotions, to discriminate among them and to use this information to guide one's thinking and actions." Emotional intelligence has been defined as the "ability to adaptively recognize emotion, express emotion, regulate emotion, and harness emotions" (Schutte, Malouff, Hall, Haggerty, Cooper, Golden, et al., 1998, 37).

Building on the research of Salovey, Mayer, and Goleman, I would like to offer this emotional intelligence (EI) development model:

Proposed Emotional Intelligence (EI) Development Model

Self-Awareness	Development Methods/Tools	Assessment Methods
Emotional self-awareness	360-degree feedback questionnaire	360-degree feedback results
Accurate self-assessment	Self-awareness survey (pre/post)	Personal observations
Self-confidence	Learning contracts	Self-awareness course scores
	Self-awareness courses/workshops	Personal interviews
	Mentors/coaches	EI survey results
	Accountability partner	
	EI survey(pre/post)	

Self-Management	Development Methods/Tools	Assessment Methods
Emotional self-control Transparency Adaptability Achievement Initiative Optimism	360-degree feedback questionnaire self-management courses/workshops facilitated role-playing exercises learning contracts (Knowles, 1975) mentors/coaches accountability partner EI survey(pre/post)	360-degree feedback results self-management course scores personal observations personal interviews EI survey results
Social Awareness	Development Methods/Tools	Assessment Methods
Empathy Organizational awareness Service	360-degree feedback questionnaire EI survey (pre/post) social awareness courses/workshops learning contracts (Knowles, 1975) intentional change theory model (Boyatzis, 2006) interviews (pre/post)	360-degree feedback results EI survey results social awareness course scores learning contracts observation personal observations personal interviews

Relationship Management	Development Methods/Tools	Assessment Methods
Inspirational leadership	360-degree feedback questionnaire	360-degree feedback results
Influence	leadership	leadership development course scores
Developing others	development courses	
Change catalyst	conflict management	EI survey results
Conflict management	courses	Conflict management
Building bonds	role-playing exercises	course scores
Teamwork/ collaboration	EI survey (pre/post)	personal observations
	relationship management courses	interviews (pre/post)

Proposed Emotional Intelligence (EI) Development Model

Based on the emotional intelligence literature and the analysis of this research, this researcher proposes the emotional intelligence development model to help facilitate the development of emotional intelligence from the primary (K–12) school to the higher education levels. This proposed emotional intelligence development model should be used in conjunction with traditional or cognitive intelligence development curricula. The cost for this proposed emotional intelligence development model may be funded from private dollars in the initial stages. However, as the program grows and expands, the expenses and costs may be allocated from current public schools' budgets. In addition, some of the funding would have to come from state and federal government sources.

In today's US educational system, the primary focus has centered on cognitive or traditional intelligence. There seems to be consensus around the fact that cognitive intelligence or abilities increase one's capacity to learn and process relevant information more rapidly and accurately (Fulmer and Barry, 2004). The results of hundreds of studies revealed two generalizations regarding cognitive intelligence. First, cognitive intelligence is predictive of individual outcomes in a wide variety of settings (e.g., educational success, occupational training success, job performance, decision-making performance, health, and social outcomes (Gottfredson, 2004). Second, cognitive intelligence provides greater practical advantages in novel or complex settings than in simpler situations (Gottfredson, 1997). Higher cognitive intelligence abilities predict better decision-making performance (LePine, Colquitt, and Erez, 2000). Cognitive intelligence abilities enable an individual to "reason, plan, solve problems, think abstractly, comprehend complex ideas, learn quickly, and learn from experience" (Gottfredson, 1997, 13). Hunter (1986) noted that cognitive intelligence abilities are related to performance itself not just to job or subject knowledge. Highly cognitively intelligent individuals are faster at cognitive operations on the job or in school settings. These highly cognitively intelligent individuals are better able to prioritize conflicting rules, and they are better at adapting old procedures to alter current situations.

With the need to develop students' emotional and social competencies, this researcher proposes the emotional intelligence development model may be used as a tool for administrators and school officials. This model is based on the framework by Goleman et al. (2002). This proposed model is called the emotional intelligence (EI) development model. The model addresses four primary emotional intelligence domains with their associated competencies. The four domains are self-awareness, self-management, social awareness, and relationship management (Goleman et al., 2002). This model provides a simple approach for emotional intelligence development, along with tools and methods to improve emotional intelligence competencies. In addition, it offers a means of assessment.

The assessment tools may be modified on an as-needed basis. However, the proposed emotional intelligence development model provides a framework that could be the genesis and catalyst for policy-makers, lawmakers, school administrators, and school officials to develop the emotional and social competencies of today's US-based students.

The proposed emotional intelligence development model is adapted from the emotional intelligence domains and competencies of Goleman et al. (2002). The development methods and tools are very practical and reasonable. In addition, the assessment methods are simple yet very helpful in ascertaining valuable and useful data points to improve the student outcomes. The emotional intelligence development models found in were adapted from Goleman et al., (2002).

Self-Awareness

Goleman et al. (2002) indicated that self-awareness included three personal competencies: 1) emotional self-awareness, 2) accurate self-assessment, and 3) self-confidence. Self-awareness is the ability to honestly reflect on and understand one's emotions, strengths, challenges, motives, values, goals, and dreams. One is able to see the big picture in a complex situation. Self-awareness helps an individual to be candid and authentic, which allows him or her to speak and express him- or herself in an open and clear manner with emotions and conviction. Self-awareness provides the primary building block for the other three domains (self-management, social awareness, and relationship management). An individual who cannot adequately know and understand him- or herself would have a difficult time trying to manage his or her own emotions, assess the emotions of others, and use that information to manage relationships with others (Goleman et al., 2002). Emotional self-awareness is the ability to read one's own emotions and recognize their impact, using one's inner signals to guide one's decisions (Goleman et al., 2002). Accurate self-assessment is the ability to know and understand one's strengths and limitations. In addition, one is able to exhibit a sense of humor about them. One is able to have a gracefulness in learning in the areas in which one needs to improve.

In essence, one is able to accept and welcome constructive criticism and feedback.

Self-confidence is defined as a sound sense of one's self-worth and capabilities. It allows an individual to have a sense of presence and self-assurance that allows him or her to stand out in a group (Goleman et al., 2002).

Self-Management

Self-management has six personal competencies: 1) self-control, 2) transparency, 3) adaptability, 4) achievement, 5) initiative, and 6) optimism. Goleman et al. (2002) noted that self-management is equated to an ongoing inner conversation and "is the component of emotional intelligence that frees us from being a prisoner of our feelings. It is what allows the mental clarity and concentrated energy that leadership demands and what keeps disruptive emotions from throwing us off track" (46). It is difficult to achieve one's personal goals and aspirations without effective self-management. Managing one's emotions and being open to others about one's feelings, beliefs, and actions helps to establish trust, integrity, and personal capital (Goleman et al., 2002).

Self-control is defined as the ability to manage disturbing emotions and impulses and to channel them in a useful way. Self-control enables one to stay calm and clear-headed under high stress or during a crisis (Goleman et. al., 2002). Transparency is the ability to display one's feelings, beliefs, and actions. This allows for integrity. Transparency helps one to openly admit mistakes or faults. In addition, transparency emboldens one to confront unethical behavior in others rather than turn a blind eye (Goleman et al., 2002).

Adaptability allows one to juggle multiple demands and priorities without losing one's focus or energy. It enables one to feel comfortable with ambiguities and difficult life situations and helps one to be flexible, nimble, and limber in the face of new challenges in life (Goleman et al., 2002). Adaptability facilitates one's ability to overcome many of life's obstacles (Goleman et al., 2002).

Achievement drives an individual to have high personal standards, which drives him or her to constantly seek performance improvements. It helps one to be pragmatic and honest about one's goals and career intentions and enables one to set challenging goals that are measurable and attainable. Achievement pushes one to continually learn and grow (Goleman et al., 2002).

Initiative is the ability of one to act and seize opportunities. Initiative allows one to create better possibilities for oneself and others. Initiative enables one to take control of one's own career intentions and destiny.

Optimism is seeing an opportunity rather than a threat in a major setback or difficulty. It allows one to positively look for the best in others. Optimism is expecting better days and outcomes in the future.

Social Awareness

Social awareness is composed of three social competencies: 1) empathy, 2) organizational awareness, and 3) service. Social awareness is defined as having the quality of being acutely aware of the emotions and needs of others. Goleman et al. (2002) indicated the following:

> By being attuned to how others feel in the moment, a leader can say and do what's appropriate—whether it be to calm fears, assuage anger, or join in good spirits. This attunement also lets a leader sense the shared values and priorities that can guide the group. (49)

In essence, social awareness enables an individual to monitor and adjust strategy, direction, and work toward accomplishing a shared vision. It helps an individual or leader to know when to push and capitalize on the momentum of the group and when to pull back and encourage reflection and collective reexamination of the purpose and priorities (Goleman et al., 2002).

Empathy is the ability to be attuned to a wide range of emotional signals that let one sense others' emotions. It helps one to understand others' perspectives and beliefs. Empathy helps one to get along with other people of diverse backgrounds and different cultures and allows one to listen very carefully to others and grasp their perspective or opinion. Organizational awareness allows one to be attuned to the organizational norms. Organizational awareness helps one to navigate and operate effectively in an environment with political and social networks and relationships. It helps one to be aware of the guiding values and unspoken rules that need to be adhered to and followed (Goleman et al., 2002).

Service fosters an emotional climate that allows one to keep relationships on the right track. It enables one to monitor and adjust to others' needs. Service helps one to stay attuned and attentive to others' desires (Goleman et al., 2002).

Relationship Management

Relationship management includes six social competencies: 1) inspiration, 2) influence, 3) developing others, 4) change catalyst, 5) conflict management, and 6) teamwork and collaboration.

Relationship management germinates from the domains of self-awareness, self-management, and social awareness, allowing the emotionally intelligent individual to effectively manage emotions perceived in others. It allows one to cultivate webs of relationships, find common ground, and use shared vision to motivate people to move forward toward accomplishing a mission or goal (Goleman et al., 2002).

Inspiration allows one to create resonance and motivates others to follow.

Resonance means that people's emotional centers are in synch in a positive way (Goleman et al., 2002).

Inspiration enables one to be a positive example to others. It helps one to articulate a shared mission and compelling vision that inspires others to follow (Goleman et al., 2002).

Influence helps one to find the right words that would appeal to others and helps one to get buy-in and acceptance from key individuals. It helps one to be persuasive and engaging when addressing a group or others.

Developing others means cultivating their abilities and competencies. It means showing a genuine interest in helping others to achieve their career intentions and life's aspirations. It means understanding and appreciating others' goals, strengths, and weaknesses. It allows one to give timely and constructive feedback to others and to become a mentor or coach.

A change catalyst allows one to recognize the need for change and challenge the status quo. It helps one to become a strong advocate and proponent for positive change even in the face of strong opposition or difficult circumstances and to overcome barriers by finding practical and pragmatic solutions (Goleman et al., 2002).

Conflict management allows one to understand and appreciate all parties' sides and perspectives. It allows one to find a common and shared solution that would appeal to all parties and helps one to address a difficult situation with boldness and conviction of purpose (Goleman et al., 2002).

Teamwork and collaboration allow one to get along with others and enable one to create an atmosphere of friendly collegiality and respect for others. Teamwork and collaboration allow for respect, helpfulness, and cooperation among people on a team. They afford the opportunity to forge and create close relationships beyond just school or work obligations (Goleman et al., 2002).

In the emotional intelligence development model, the development methods and tools that are proposed include the following items: a 360-degree feedback questionnaire, a self-awareness survey (pre/post), learning contracts, self-awareness courses and workshops, mentors and coaches, an accountability partner, and an emotional intelligence survey (pre/post). The 360-degree feedback questionnaire would help the students to understand how they are viewed from others' perspectives. This development method would be valuable to developing the student's sense of self-awareness and self-confidence. The student would have a genuine understanding of his or her competencies and abilities. When the student's behavioral weaknesses and strengths have been identified, a learning contract could be used to either systematically change or keep the student's behaviors.

The self-awareness survey would be given to students and their parent or guardian in the primary to high school grade levels. The students and their parent or guardian would be responsible for completing the self-awareness survey before the start of a school year. In addition, they would be responsible for completing the self-awareness survey after the school year. Each year, the students and the school administrators would be responsible for reviewing the self-awareness survey results in a private manner. The annual self-awareness reviews would build accountability into the process. The learning contracts would be used to develop a plan of action for the individual student. Each student would agree to a learning contract between the teachers, parents, and themselves. The learning contracts would be used in the primary to high school grade levels.

At the college level, learning contracts could be used by first-year college students and their professors. Self-awareness courses and workshops would serve to educate the students on the essentials of self-awareness. These courses should be mandatory in the primary to high school levels. At the college level, the self-awareness courses and workshop should be optional. Mentors and coaches should be identified and provided to any student from the primary to the college levels who wants one. The mentors and coaches would serve as role models and examples. They would create a sense of community around the student.

The accountability partner could be a fellow student. He or she is responsible for ensuring that the student stays on track to achieve his or her goals.

The emotional intelligence survey (pre/post) should be used to identify which specific emotional intelligence competencies are strong and which are weak. The emotional intelligence survey should be completed by the student at the beginning and end of the academic school year. It should be completed by students in the primary to high school levels and in the first year of college or university.

In the proposed emotional intelligence development model, the following assessment methods should be used: 360-degree feedback results, personal observations, self-awareness courses scores, personal interviews, emotional intelligence survey results, self-management course scores, social awareness course scores, learning contract observation, leadership development course scores, and conflict management course scores. The 360-degree feedback results provide a barometer of how the student is perceived and viewed by others. When these results are provided to students from the primary to the college levels, they give them a realistic view of how they are perceived by others. The students may use the feedback to modify and change their behavior. The personal observations would be administrated by a trained behavior professional. The personal observations would serve as a means to monitor the student's behavior in a safe and normal environment. Personal observations would be done on a voluntary basis from the primary grades to the first year of college.

The self-awareness course scores would be used to identify how the students are progressing. In addition, they would be able to observe their own progress and determine which behaviors need to be changed or modified. The personal interviews would be done in conjunction with the personal observations. The personal interviews would provide a qualitative research approach for identifying and developing the students' behavioral needs. The personal interviews would be completed in a voluntary and confidential manner. The emotional intelligence survey results would serve as a vehicle to improve the emotional intelligence competencies of the students from the primary to the first-year college level.

The students would be provided their emotional intelligence survey results at the start and end of an academic school year. They would be able to track their emotional intelligence competence development. The self-management course and social awareness scores would be used to see if the students comprehend and understand the course material. The scores would be compiled and provided to the students from the primary to the first-year college level. The learning contract observation would be used to see if the students have written down their learning contract. In addition, the learning observation would serve as a conversation starter between the students and the observers. If the students need assistance with the learning contract, the observers would direct them to the appropriate area. The leadership development course scores would serve to show whether the students are grasping the primary leadership skills and competencies from the course material. The leadership development course and conflict management scores should be collected, compiled, and shared with the students from the primary to the first year of college.

Research Questions

Research Question 1: What is the association between the emotional intelligence of first-year college students and their career intentions to complete their college degrees?

Research Question 2: What is the correlation between the emotional intelligence of first-year international college students and their career intentions to complete their college degrees?

Hypothesis HO[1] (Null Hypothesis): There will be no significant association between emotional intelligence (EIS) and first-year college students' career intentions to complete their degrees (CCI).

Hypothesis HA¹ (Alternative Hypothesis): There is a statistically positive association between emotional intelligence (EIS) and first-year college students' career intentions to complete their degree (CCI).

Hypothesis HO² (Null Hypothesis): There will be no significant difference between academic majors of study on emotional intelligence scores.

Hypothesis HA² (Alternative Hypothesis): There will be a significant difference between academic majors of study on emotional intelligence scores.

Conceptual/Theoretical Framework

For this study, the two theoretical frameworks that would be used are the Schutte, Malouff, Hall, Haggerty, Cooper, Golden, et al. (1998) Emotional Intelligence Scale (EIS) and Larson, Heppner, Ham, and Dugan's (1988) Coping with Career Indecision (CCI) scale. Schutte et al.'s (1998) Emotional Intelligence Scale (EIS) is a self-report measure that includes thirty-three items. In some literature, the Emotional Intelligence Scale is called the Assessing Emotions Scale. In addition, it is referred to as the Self-Report Emotional Intelligence Test or the Schutte Emotional Intelligence Scale (Schutte, Malouff, and Bhullar, 2009).

To measure the ability of first-year college students' career intentions to cope with career indecision, a modified version of the Coping with Career Indecision (CCI) scale will be used (Larson et al., 1988).

CHAPTER 10

DEFINITIONS

This exploratory quantitative study will only recruit and use study participants from one Midwestern college for its sample set. Future research should incorporate a wider sample of participants. Future research should use a qualitative approach and more in-depth data to get more raw data from the study participants. In addition, future research needs to examine the association between emotional intelligence, work experience, and other individual-level variables, such as conscientiousness, that might have an important effect (Shipley, Jackson, and Segrest, 2010).

Definition of Terms

- *Baby boomers*—an American citizen born between the years of 1946 to 1964 (Peters, 2010)
- *Community college*—a two-year institution of higher learning. It meets the training needs of the subbaccalaureate section of the workforce (Grubb, Badway, Bell, and Castellano, 2000)
- *Coping with Career Indecision scale*—a self-report measure that includes thirty-five items. It is commonly called CCI (Larson, Heppner, Ham, and Dugan, 1988)
- *Emotional Intelligence*—the ability to recognize and understand emotions and the skill to use this awareness to manage oneself and one's associations with others (Goleman, 1995)
- *Emotional Intelligence Scale*—a self-report measure that includes thirty-three items. It is also called the Assessing Emotional Scale or the Schutte Emotional Intelligence Scale (Schutte, Malouff, and Bhullar, 2009).

- *Globalization*—manifested in the freer and more large-scale mobility of capital and people between economies and societies, triggering political and cultural exchanges (Lasonen, 2005)
- *Nontraditional student*—includes individuals who have not followed a continuous educational path into college (Newbold, Mehta, and Forbus, 2010)
- *Selected Control*—involves two defining processes; first, it refers to engaging in the pursuit of chosen goals and trying to change one's environment so that goals can be achieved; second, it refers to internal processes that enhance the motivation to pursue the goal by creating favorable representations to the goal and one's ability to pursue it (Schindler and Tomasik, 2010)
- *Self-leadership*—consists of a variety of interwoven strategies that address individuals' self-awareness, volition, motivation, cognition, and behavior (Manz and Neck, 1991)
- *Self-talk*—means of enhancing self-awareness and self-regulation, both of which are considered important in the construct of emotional intelligence (Depape, Hakim-Larson, Voelker, Page, and Jackson, 2008)

Summary

Locke (1999) articulated that improving the economic and social conditions for a community or a particular group in the United States has always been linked to education. With the advances in technology and the globalization of society, postsecondary education or training is increasingly becoming a must. According to the Education Trust (1999), state education CEOs investigating the gap between high school graduation and college or high-performance jobs stated that:

Our nation is no longer well served by an education system that prepares a few to attend college to develop their minds for learned pursuits while the rest are expected only to build their muscles for useful labor. In the twenty-first century, all students must meet higher achievement standards in elementary, secondary, and postsecondary schools and thus be better prepared for the challenges of work and citizenship. (Locke, 1999)

Success in today's global society demands that employees possess at least the skills and knowledge required of a high school graduate if they are to be competitive in the workforce of the twenty-first century and beyond. Failure to meet this minimum requirement, however, limits the economic and social potential for millions of young Americans each year (Hayes, Nelson, Tabin, Pearson, and Worthy, 2002; US Department of Education, 1999). The value of the college degree in a global society is very important to the community student. Therefore, this research will explore and examine the association between emotional intelligence and first-year college students' career intentions to complete their degrees. The data from this research will be shared with the academic community.

CHAPTER 11

EMOTIONAL INTELLIGENCE DEVELOPMENT

In management training, the aim of development efforts is to help people become more effective. It requires development of competencies, as well as arousal of the appropriate motivation and value drivers. The question is whether the methods are effective or not (Banta, 1993; Mentkowski, 2000; Pascarella and Terenzini, 1991; Winter, McClelland, and Stewart, 1981).

Boyatzis (2009) noted that the concept of competency and the nascent area of emotional and social intelligence competencies (ESCs) have evolved into a flexible framework for the selection, assessment, and development of human talent in organizations all over the world. Emotional intelligence competency is an ability to recognize, understand, and use emotional information about oneself and others that leads to or causes effective or superior performance.. And a cognitive intelligence competency is an ability to think about or analyze information and situations that leads to or causes effective or superior performance (Boyatzis, 2009). Emmerling and Boyatzis (2012) emphasized that ESCs are "learned capabilities based on emotional intelligence which results in superior performance" (8). This helps to underscore a distinction in the prediction of work performance (Emmerling and Boyatzis, 2012).

Beyond knowledge and competencies, the additional ingredient necessary for outstanding performance appeared to be the desire to use one's talent. This seems driven by a person's values, philosophy, sense of calling or mission, and unconscious motives and traits (Boyatzis, 2006; Boyatzis and Sala, 2004). The motives and traits affected the way a person saw the world, especially the perception of opportunities and challenges he or she perceived in the environment. However, they also are persistent a generalized drivers. They aroused dispositional ways a person responded to his or her environment and created a focus for a person's behavior.

These three domains of capability or talent helped in understanding what a person can do (i.e., knowledge), how a person can do it (i.e., competencies), and why a person feels the need to do it (i.e., values, motives, and unconscious dispositions). Our role in management education is to help people add value on each of these domains—to help them to prepare to be effective in future jobs and careers.

The researchers indicated that one of the primary objectives of training and graduate management education is to prepare people to be outstanding managers, leaders, and professionals. To understand what graduate students may be learning requires a model of human talent and an understanding of what the workplace needs for effective performance in terms of that mode (Boyatzis and Saatcioglu, 2008).

McEnrue, Groves, and Shen (2009) noted that an individual's predisposition to seek and utilize feedback is an important factor when considering which individuals are likely to benefit from emotional intelligence training or other leadership development educational programs. Receptivity to feedback is a significant predictor of emotional intelligence training gains. Receptivity to feedback plays a large role in the effort to develop potential leaders' emotional intelligence (McEnrue, Groves, and Shen, 2009).

Yuvaraj and Srivastava (2007) indicated that the role of emotions in the workplace was probably first underscored and documented by Hochschild, who researched the effects of emotional labor in service industries (Hochschild, 1983). Goleman (1998) indicated that emotional intelligence concepts may apply to the workplace environment. He noted that the emotionally intelligent worker is skilled in two areas. The two areas are personal competence and social competence. The personal competence refers to how individuals manage themselves. The social competence refers how individuals manage relationships.

Globalization

The global landscape has changed for many of today's college students. The business world has become more global and connected. Lasonen (2005) asserted that globalization has manifested in the freer and more large-scale mobility of capital and people between economies and societies, triggering political and cultural exchanges. Globalization gradually creates new kinds of social realities. Both individuals and societies come under pressure. This opens new avenues of action (Lasonen, 2005). The pressures globalization generates can be addressed by emphasizing competence across the whole range of educational provision and forms of knowledge production and application from basic education to higher education and to research and product development of a high standard (Lasonen, 2005).

Ferdig, Coutts, DiPietro, and Lok (2007) indicated that there are many aspects of becoming a global citizen. One of the most important areas is an awareness and understanding of the variety and relevance of all cultures. Intercultural awareness is important to college students. Education with the aim of promoting intercultural dialogue and understanding has the additional goal of training people to act. One is able to adopt a cooperative approach, as a mediator and interpreter between different cultures and their citizens (Lasonen, 2005).

Vayrynen (1997) noted that globalization is different from internationalization. The term *internationalization* covers interdependence between countries guided by national policies. However, internationalization is both a process parallel to globalization and a step toward it (Vayrynen, 1997).

Today's college students must be equipped with a college degree or education to be a productive member of the global society. By employing emotional intelligence theory and exercises, they will become well-rounde graduates. These graduates will have a solid foundation in the knowle and skills they will need to be productive global managers and le (Tucker, Sojka, Barone, and McCarthy, 2000).

Reginald Ramsey, PhD, MBA, CISA

Decision-Making Process

A considerable body of behavioral research concerned with organizational behavior addresses the process of decision-making among college youth. Many of these individuals will someday fill administrative positions in a variety of future careers. In most cases, individuals want to make good decisions for the betterment of themselves and their institutions. Therefore, it is a good idea to study this area. Staw (1976) suggests that decision makers often resist change and that organizations often maintain old ways even when faced with failure. In addition, some organizations may actually intensify their commitment to a failing program by "throwing good money after bad" (Moore, Jensen, and Hauck, 1990).

Moore, Jensen, and Hauck (1990) indicated that two theoretical models support the suggestion that decision-making is not always based on rational thought. The "conflict theory" asserts that anxiety and stress can determine conditions wherein administrators either make good choices or make things worse through efforts to reduce their own anxiety (Janis, 1982).

The other theory is called the "justification model." This model holds that individuals attempt to justify and rationalize past decisions, especially poor ones, in order to maintain self-esteem (Fox and Staw, 1979). Janis and Mann (1976) indicated that decision makers react differently to stressful or threatening situations. In efforts to reduce anxiety, one individual may choose "deference avoidance" behavior by rationalizing, while another individual may display "decisional vigilance" by becoming aroused to seek new and vital information and rethink alternatives. What makes students continue with their educational aspirations and complete their degrees in spite of life's difficulties?

Career Intentions

Gati, Krausz, and Osipow (1996) indicated that college students needed to be informed about the career decision process and ways of resolving psychological difficulties they may encounter during this process. A possible first step for enhancing career counseling is to classify the career-related problems of students (Osipow and Winer, 1996). This classification can provide the information needed to establish differentiated intervention strategies that cater to the individual needs of students. There is a diverse array of tools available for this process including

a) a screening device for clients who need career counseling (Meyer and Winer, 1993)

b) an analysis for identifying diverse problems according to sex differences (Burns, 1994)

c) an information guide to determine the focus of the intervention program for career improvement (Haislett and Hafer, 1990)

d) criteria for evaluating career counseling outcomes (Mau and Jepsen, 1992)

Lee (2005) asserted that in career decision-making, students are typically classified into two groups in the literature: "decided" or "undecided." However, some researchers have suggested that undecided students should not be treated as a homogeneous group. Rather, they point out the need to classify them into subtypes according to more specific factors (Chartrand, Robbins, Morrill, and Boggs, 1990); Larson, Heppner, Ham, and Dugan, 1988). Some of the subtypes are outlined in Gianakos (1999) and Bluestein (1989). Gianakos (1999) suggested four types of career choice including stable, conventional, multiple-trial, and unstable. Bluestein (1989) developed a typology composed of stable, explorator~ and unstable types. The typologies have been empirically validated employing career instruments such as the Career Decision Scale (Osi

1987), My Vocational Situation (Holland, Daiger, and Power, 1980), and the Career Factor Inventory (Chartrand et al., 1990).

Peterson, Sampson, Lenz, and Reardon (2002) theorized that poor career problem-solving and decision-making skills are related to negative thinking or dysfunctional career thoughts, and they developed the Career Thoughts Inventory (CTI) in 1996 to measure such thoughts. Today, researchers are seeking to learn more about dysfunctional career thoughts and how they relate to other constructs important in career decision-making, including communication apprehension. Previous studies have found dysfunctional career thoughts to be significantly correlated with the inability to choose a major field of study (Kilk, 1997), a level of attention-deficit/hyperactivity disorder (Painter, 2004), and depression and career indecision (Saunders, Sampson, Peterson, and Reardon, 2000). College students with higher levels of dysfunctional career thoughts do not appear to make a positive adjustment to their learning disability (Dipeolu, Reardon, Sampson, and Burkhead, 2002), and individuals with cognitive impairments have more decision-making confusion and external conflict than do individuals with physical disabilities (Yanchak, Lease, and Strauser, 2005).

Selected Control

Schindler and Tomasik (2010) indicated that humans are inherently motivated to control their environment and to invest their resources in courses of action that allow maintaining and enhancing their capacity for control (Heckhausen, 1999, 2000; Heckhausen and Schulz, 1995). This control striving is expressed in people trying to secure a fulfilling and well-paying job or establishing a close and satisfying association with a romantic partner. To succeed in such endeavors, individuals need to select appropriate life paths and goals and refrain from inappropriate goals on which control striving would be wasted.

Schindler and Tomasik (2010) studied career and association decisions of college students between eighteen and twenty-five years. This phase of emerging adulthood has been characterized as "the age of possibilities" (Arnett, 2004; Heckhausen, 1999), where individuals still have time to experiment and figure out their choices in the areas of work and love. Schindler and Tomasik (2010) used the life-span theory of control (Heckhausen, 1999; Heckhausen and Schulz, 1995) as a framework for their study. This theory identifies two basic requirements that human behavior needs to fulfill in order to be effective: the management of selectivity and the compensation for failure experiences. The theory further defines two corresponding types of control strategies (selective and compensatory control).

The functionality of employing these control strategies varies with the opportunities afforded by a person's context as has been shown for different life domains including career development and family/intimate associations (Heckhausen and Tomasik, 2002; Wrosch and Heckhausen, 1999). When opportunities for achieving one's goals are favorable, employing selective control strategies leads to positive outcomes. In contrast, compensatory control strategies proved adaptive with unattainable goals and foregone opportunities. The participants had comparably favorable opportunities for choosing a college major or a romantic partner. Selective control striving is required because of the great flexibility and scope of human behavior combined with individuals' limited resources for action (e.g., time, effort, skills) (Schindler and Tomasik, 2010).

It is impossible to pursue all available opportunities; humans need to focus their investment of resources on the attainment of selected goals and life paths—to select specific behavioral options and to protect subsequently the selected options against competing action tendencies. Selective control involves two defining processes. First, selective control means engaging in the pursuit of chosen goals and trying to change one's environment so that goals can be achieved. Second, selective control refers to internal proces that enhance the motivation to pursue the goal by creating favorable representations of the goal and one's ability to pursue it. Such selective control strategies can be applied when choosing life paths (complete a college degree). When choosing a college major, using selective control strategies means investing energy and effort in collecting and evaluating information on possible majors and in remaining focused on the decision that needs to be made. If successful, this should help identify a self-evident choice (Schindler and Tomasik, 2010).

Positive correlations were found between participants' reported use of selected control strategies when making important life choices in general and their satisfaction with their subsequently chosen college major. Selected control was unrelated to satisfaction with the college major decision process. The perceived attractiveness of to-be-chosen college majors significantly increased between four months before the choice and the time of choice while the perceived attractiveness of to-be-rejected majors declined. In addition, participants further varied in the perceived attractiveness of their chosen and non-chosen majors at the time of choice. This was due to the sample size (Schindler and Tomasik, 2010).

CHAPTER 12

SUMMARY AND CONCLUSION

Salovey and Mayer (1990) first used the expression "emotional intelligence." They indicated that emotional intelligence included an "ability to monitor one's own and others' feelings and emotions, to discriminate among them and to use this information to guide one's thinking and actions" (189).

Goleman (1998) presented a model of emotional intelligence by using twenty-five competencies arrayed in five clusters. The five clusters included self-awareness, self-regulation, motivation, empathy, and social skills. The clusters indicated the behavioral groups of the desired competencies.

Christie, Jordan, Troth, and Lawrence (2007) noted that the emotional intelligence construct is still the focus of substantial controversy. The controversy surrounded two schools of thought. Goleman (1995; 1998) argued that emotional intelligence consists of a number of social and emotional competencies that includes self-motivation. Mayer and Salovey (1997) articulated that emotional intelligence abilities are restricted to abilities that directly link emotions to cognition and that motivation is not a factor. Mayer and Salovey (1997) proposed that emotional intelligence is a higher-order concept composed of four iterative dimensions that included emotional awareness, facilitating emotion, understanding emotion, and managing emotions.

Goleman (2001) revised his emotional intelligence framework to four ability clusters. The abilities are similar to those of the previous model. However, they are grouped as self-awareness, self-management, social awareness, and association management. Goleman maintained that motivation stemmed from internal mechanisms rather than external sources.

Emotional intelligence development entails the development

competencies. Boyatzis (2009) indicated that the concept of competency and the nascent field of emotional and social intelligence competencies (ESCs) have evolved into a flexible framework for the selection, assessment, and development of human talent in organizations all over the world. An additional ingredient necessary to outstanding performance appears to be the desire to use one's talent (Boyatzis, 2006).

Lasonen (2005) noted that globalization has manifested in the freer and more large-scale mobility of capital and people between economies and societies, triggering political and cultural exchanges. This opens new avenues of action. Today's college students must be equipped with a college degree or education to be a productive member of the global society. Today's college students must apply emotional intelligence theory and exercises to become well-rounded graduates. College students need to be informed about the career decision process and ways of resolving psychological difficulties they may encounter during this process (Gati, Krausz, and Osipow, 1996).

Today's college students need emotional intelligence competencies to compete in the global marketplace. In addition, employers require that their college recruits have higher levels of personal and interpersonal skills (Porter and McKibbin, 1988). Goleman (1995) indicated that emotional intelligence might play a role in developing personal and interpersonal skills. The purpose of this study is to examine if there is a significant association between emotional intelligence and first-year college students' career intentions to complete their degree.

This book is dedicated and targeted to the millions of junior high school, senior high school, and college students globally who are interested in successfully transitioning from their humble beginnings (blue collar) home environment to working for a large global organization (white collar) (e.g., corporate America, global organization, large governmental organization, and so on).

As I was rereading the book *The Measure of a Man*, by Dr. Martin

Luther King, Jr., I came across this poem by John Oxenham. Personally, I love the words and lesson in this poem. As you read the poem, please think and reflect on it. The poem is entitled "The Ways."

> To every man there openeth
> A Way, and Ways, and a Way.
> And the High Soul climbs the High way,
> And the Low Soul gropes the Low,
> And in between, on the misty flats,
> The rest drift to and fro.
> But to every man there openeth
> A High Way, and a Low.
> And every man decideth
> The Way his soul shall go.

Over my career, I have shared these valuable words of wisdom to my mentees, students, or other individuals who wanted to understand how to succeed in their chosen fields of endeavor. In this book, I am sharing with you some tools and techniques that helped me to successfully navigate from a blue-collar home environment to the white-collar corporate environment.

In this book, I shared what worked, what did not work, and lessons that I learned from my personal experience. Personally, I want you to use the tools that work for you and discard or not use the tools or techniques that do not work for you. In addition, if you need to adjust or modify the tool or technique to your personality, I am fine with that as well. Please use this book as your guide and personal development tool.

Remember to enjoy your transition from the blue-collar to the white-collar ranks. Moreover, please, do not ever forget where you came from. Many of us come from humble beginnings. Let's continue to reach back and help those individuals who are coming behind us. They need our wisdom, knowledge, and insight. Please, pay it forward.

My purpose is for you to think and decide how you can becom

best person that you are ordained to become. In addition, I want you to successfully transition from your humble or blue-collar beginnings to the professional world or white-collar business environment. I believe in you. I know that you can achieve whatever you set as your goal. However, you must start today! Change is a process. It takes time to change.

Throughout this book, you may have observed that I made many mistakes, errors, and bad decisions over my career. However, the one thing that I did right was that I did not let one mistake or one bad decision deter or stop me from moving forward. You see, I believe that I am special. I am here on the earth for a reason. I believe that God has placed me on this earth for a special purpose. As a matter of fact, I believe each of us is placed on this earth for a special purpose or a special reason if you will. We just have to find what that special purpose is for us. However, we all are needed and wanted on this earth. I truly believe this to be true.

One of my reasons for living is to share my personal and work experiences in this book with you. In this book, you will find words of wisdom, knowledge, passion, and love. I hope and pray that you will glean some knowledge to help you. My friend, I love serving others. And I love to see others succeed. It makes me happy. Also, I love it when someone I have helped throughout their career comes back to me and says, "Dr. Ramsey, what you said X number of years ago changed my life." From my standpoint, this is my reward.

In addition, I love to see my mentees and students do well and be in positions of authority and power, where they are able to share some of my wisdom, knowledge, or words with others. This is my reward too. We are put on this earth to be of service to each other. We need each other. I strongly believe that.

Therefore, as you read this book, keep in mind, it is a book that I want you to use, carry with you, and review over and over. I believe as ¡ read, study, and meditate on some of the words in this book, you will ge your thinking. As you change your thinking, you will change your behavior. As your behavior changes, your habits and friends will change as well. I pray and hope that you share this wisdom with others. That is the best reward.

How did this book come about? That is a great question. This book is the product of many years of starting and stopping. I started writing this book at the age of around thirty. Now, I am fifty-four years of age. As you can see, I have been writing this book for over twenty years. Most books are written much faster than that. However, I had to experience and learn more things before I could seriously sit down and express my words and thoughts in writing. In addition, the process of writing is very hard and cumbersome for me. I am pretty good at speaking, but the discipline to sit down and write is very arduous for me. However, I strongly believe that this book is needed in today's complex, crazy, and global world.

When I began my professional career, I wish I had a book like this one that I could have used to help me with my transition from my blue-collar thought process to a white-collar thinking mentality. Personally, the only thing that I had was my parents', grandparents', and other family's and friends' teachings and thoughts on how to succeed in an environment that they did not know or understand in a professional way. They shared with me what they knew. However, most of them did not have any experience working in a white-collar environment. Most of them shared their blue-collar experience and knowledge with me. I began to see from my experience that their good intentions were not helping me to grow and prosper in the white-collar environment. I needed to learn both the written and unwritten rules of how to successfully navigate this new white-collar terrain.

In other words, I had to learn new ways to successfully communicate and work more effectively and efficiently. I needed to learn how to work smarter, not harder. This was a major thought process change from wh[...] I was taught as a child. As a child, I was taught to "do a good j[...] and someone would see it and reward you." This sounds good in th[...]

However, in the white-collar world, this philosophy did not work too well for me. Therefore, I needed to learn a new and different philosophy that would help me to succeed in this new world of white-collar thinking.

For my 2014 personal goals, I set a goal to complete this book. I got very serious and wrote nearly every day, but I was not able to achieve my goal.

However, in August 2017, I reset my personal book goal to completing this book by August 2018. I did it! This is a dream come true. I hope and pray that you will find this book to be of value to you.

In addition, if you would like to discuss or debate some of the points in this book, please contact my publisher or me directly. I would love to come to you or to your group to share my reasoning and thought process with you. I am confident that you and I would be able to come to a reasonable solution. Please, give me your honest and sincere feedback. I cherish and respect your opinions and thoughts on this book. You never know, I may use some of your feedback (both positive and constructive) for my next book.

As you read this book, please keep an open mind and willing spirit. I sincerely want you to successfully navigate the transition from a blue-collar home environment to the white-collar thinking and mentality. My view is that one must change one's thinking and mentality to successfully transition from the blue-collar to the white-collar world. As you read this book, you will see why I stated this point. In brief, it is a process to change your thinking and mentality. It will not come overnight or quickly. You must work at it on a daily and regular basis. It takes time, effort, focus, discipline, perseverance, and a sincere desire to change.

However, I believe in *you*. I believe that *you* can do anything that you set your mind to do. I believe that *you* are special. I believe that your past does not define or determine your future. You can become the person that *you* want to become. It takes daily and deliberate steps to make that change. However, I know and believe that *you* can do it! Now, let's get to work!

The first part of your change is for you to read, study, and meditate on the lessons and words from this book. After that, you need to apply what you have learned in your daily activities. You can change and become the best *you* that you were born to become. I know this from my own personal experience.

APPENDIX A

The Assessing Emotions Scale

Directions: *Your completion of this survey implies consent to participate in this research.* Each of the following items asks you about your emotions or reactions associated with emotions. After deciding whether a statement is generally true for you, use the five-point scale to respond to the statement. Please circle "1" if you strongly disagree that this is like you, "2" if you somewhat disagree that this is like you, "3" if you neither agree nor disagree that this is like you, "4" if you somewhat agree that this is like you, and "5" if you strongly agree that this is like you.

There are no right or wrong answers. Please give the response that best describes you.

> 1 = strongly disagree
> 2 = somewhat disagree
> 3 = neither agree nor disagree
> 4 = somewhat agree
> 5 = strongly agree

1. I know when to speak about my personal problems to others. 1 2 3 4 5
2. When I am faced with obstacles, I remember times I faced similar obstacles and overcame them. 1 2 3 4 5
3. I expect that I will do well on most things I try. 1 2 3 4 5
4. Other people find it easy to confide in me. 1 2 3 4 5
5. I find it hard to understand the nonverbal messages of other people. 1 2 3 4 5
6. Some of the major events of my life have led me to reevaluate what is important and not important. 1 2 3 4 5

7. When my mood changes, I see new possibilities. 1 2 3 4 5

8. Emotions are one of the things that make my life worth living. 1 2 3 4 5

9. I am aware of my emotions as I experience them. 1 2 3 4 5

10. I expect good things to happen. 1 2 3 4 5

11. I like to share my emotions with others. 1 2 3 4 5

12. When I experience a positive emotion, I know how to make it last. 1 2 3 4 5

13. I arrange events others enjoy. 1 2 3 4 5

14. I seek out activities that make me happy. 1 2 3 4 5

15. I am aware of the nonverbal messages I send to others. 1 2 3 4 5

16. I present myself in a way that makes a good impression on others. 1 2 3 4 5

17. When I am in a positive mood, solving problems is easy for me. 1 2 3 4 5

18. By looking at their facial expressions, I recognize the emotions people are experiencing. 1 2 3 4 5

19. I know why my emotions change. 1 2 3 4 5

20. When I am in a positive mood, I am able to come up with new ideas. 1 2 3 4 5

21. I have control over my emotions. 1 2 3 4 5

22. I easily recognize my emotions as I experience them. 1 2 3 4 5

23. I motivate myself by imagining a good outcome to tasks I take on. 1 2 3 4 5

24. I compliment others when they have done something well. 1 2 3 4 5

25. I am aware of the nonverbal messages other people send. 1 2 3 4 5

26. When another person tells me about an important event in his or her life, I almost feel as though I experienced this event myself. 1 2 3 4 5

27. When I feel a change in emotions, I tend to come up with new ideas.   1 2 3 4 5

28. When I am faced with a challenge, I give up because I believe I will fail.   1 2 3 4 5

29. I know what other people are feeling just by looking at them.   1 2 3 4 5

30. I help other people feel better when they are down.   1 2 3 4 5

31. I use good moods to help myself keep trying in the face of obstacles.   1 2 3 4 5

32. I can tell how people are feeling by listening to the tone of their voice.   1 2 3 4 5

33. It is difficult for me to understand why people feel the way they do.   1 2 3 4 5

APPENDIX B

CCI Scale (modified)

Directions: Indicate the extent to which you agree or disagree with the following thirty-five questions. (Circle one response for each item.) After deciding whether a statement is generally true for you, use the six-point scale to respond to the statement. Please circle "1" if you *strongly agree* that this is like you, "2" if you *moderately agree* that this is like you, "3" if you *slightly agree* that this is like you, "4" if you *slightly disagree* that this is like you, "5" if you *moderately disagree* that this is like you, and "6" if you *strongly disagree* that this is like you.

Please remember, there are no right or wrong answers.

1= Strongly agree
2= Moderately agree
3= Slightly agree
4= Slightly disagree
5= Moderately disagree
6= Strongly disagree

1. I feel a lot of pressure from my parents to choose a certain major and/or career. 1 2 3 4 5 6
2. I am confident in my ability to succeed academically in the courses necessary to enter my chosen or potential career. 1 2 3 4 5 6
3. If graduate school were necessary for pursuing a career, I am confident that I would be accepted and do well. 1 2 3 4 5 6
4. I have a high degree of math ability. 1 2 3 4 5 6
5. I have a high degree of academic ability. 1 2 3 4 5 6

6. A career decision at this point is so important because it determines what I will be doing for the rest of my life. 1 2 3 4 5 6

7. It is essential to choose the right major now so that I don't have to change later and waste time and money. 1 2 3 4 5 6

8. People with good jobs are almost always happy. 1 2 3 4 5 6

9. I feel as if I have too many interests to settle on any one field. 1 2 3 4 5 6

10. If I could find the right career, many of my other personal problems would be solved. 1 2 3 4 5 6

11. I need to identify right away what skills and abilities I have. 1 2 3 4 5 6

12. Finances limit what career choice I make. 1 2 3 4 5 6

13. An influential person doesn't approve of my career choice, which is hindering me from seeking that career. 1 2 3 4 5 6

14. I don't have the special talents to follow my first career choice. 1 2 3 4 5 6

15. I often feel that my life lacks much purpose. 1 2 3 4 5 6

16. I know little about what kinds of people enter different occupations. 1 2 3 4 5 6

17. I know a lot about the typical duties of jobs that interest me. 1 2 3 4 5 6

18. I know the types of careers in which I could perform well. 1 2 3 4 5 6

19. It seems like I receive a lot of contradictory or confusing information on academic majors that I have considered. 1 2 3 4 5 6

20. I spend time every day thinking about a major and career and what I might do about it. 1 2 3 4 5 6

21. I have a clear idea how to go about choosing a major (field of study) and selecting a career. 1 2 3 4 5 6

22. At this point in time, almost any major would be   1 2 3 4 5 6
    better than no major.

23. I have *actively* persisted by *doing something* to help me   1 2 3 4 5 6
    select a major and career.

24. I tend to smooth over any career indecision and   1 2 3 4 5 6
    pretend that it doesn't exist.

25. I tend to procrastinate or avoid selecting a major and   1 2 3 4 5 6
    career and just let time run its course.

26. I frequently blame myself for something I did or did   1 2 3 4 5 6
    not do in selecting a major or career.

27. I often feel down or depressed about selecting a major   1 2 3 4 5 6
    or career.

28. I often hope that any problems I have or have had in   1 2 3 4 5 6
    selecting my major and career would just disappear.

29. I often feel a sense of helplessness in selecting a major   1 2 3 4 5 6
    and planning my career.

30. I think that I should make a career decision as soon   1 2 3 4 5 6
    as possible, but I can't and this makes me anxious.

31. I get worried when I think about the intense   1 2 3 4 5 6
    competition in most careers.

32. I find it difficult to make decisions in general, no   1 2 3 4 5 6
    matter what issue is involved.

33. I have looked for information (e.g., have read books   1 2 3 4 5 6
    or taken particular classes) that have helped me make
    a decision regarding a major and career.

34. I have an adequate amount of information to make   1 2 3 4 5 6
    a career decision.

35. I feel stress or pressure in selecting a satisfying major   1 2 3 4 5 6
    and career.

APPENDIX C

Research Instruments

EIS

The model proposed that emotional intelligence consists of appraisal of emotion in the self and others, expression of emotion, regulation of emotion in the self and others, and utilization of emotion in solving problems. It was development using the Emotional Intelligence Scale (EIS). In addition, other branches include functions such as verbal and nonverbal appraisal and expression of emotion and using emotions to motivate as part of the utilization of emotions (Schutte, Malouff, and Bhullar, 2009).

Evidence has been found for the measure's reliability and validity in adults from both university and community settings. The measure was constructed based on the model of emotional intelligence proposed by Salovey and Mayer (1990). Participants respond to each item using a five-point scale, with 1 as "strongly disagree," 2 as "somewhat disagree," 3 as "neither agree nor disagree," 4 as "somewhat agree," and 5 as "strongly agree" (Schutte et al., 1998). This measure yields a global score ranging from 33 to 165, with higher scores indicating greater emotional intelligence (Schutte et al., 1998). The reliability and validity of data collected from the measure in the internal consistency of the thirty-three-item scale was found to be .90 for a sample of university and community adults. Two-week test-retest reliability was reported at .78 for university students. Schutte and Malouff (1998) found that higher EIS scores were related to greater self-monitoring and empathy. Several studies have reported means and standard deviations on the total scale scores from men and women separately. Generally, these studies have found that women score somewhat higher on the measure than men. In some studies, this difference has bee statistically significant (Carmeli and Josman, 2006; Schutte et al., 1998). In other studies, the difference has not been statistically significant (Saklofske et al., 2003; Schutte, Malouff, Bobik, Coston, Greeson, Jedlicka, Rhodes, and Wendorf, 2001; Wing, Schutte and Byrne, 2006). Factor analyses performed on the EIS has resulted in four subscales. The subscales identified by Ciarrochi, Chan, and Bajgar (2001) were perception, managing others' emotions, managing self-relevant emotions, and utilizing emotions, with alpha coefficient reliabilities of .76, .66, .63, and .55, respectively. The alpha coefficient for overall emotional intelligence (sum of all thirty-three items) was .84.

The items for the original assessing emotions scale or EIS were in English (Schutte et al., 1998). Most studies utilize the English-language version of the scale. However, some studies have used translations of the scale. Carmeli (2003) used a Hebrew version of the scale. Oginska-Bulik (2005) used a Polish version of the scale. Sjoberg (2001) used a Swedish version of the scale. In addition, Yurtsever (2003) used a Turkish version of the scale. The scale was first developed and validated as an English-language scale (Schutte et al., 1998), and the majority of studies use the scale focused on participants from English-speaking countries.

CCI

Schutte et al. (1998) suggested that the Coping with Career Indecision (CCI) scale might appropriately be used for research purposes and to assist individuals who are motivated to self-reflect on aspects of their emotional functioning in the context of issues such as career goals or the experience of problems that may be related to emotional functioning. As the items on the scale are transparent and respondents may perceive some answers as more socially desirable than others. The scale is based on the definition put forth in the original Salovey and Mayer (1990) model.

The CCI scale uses a scale ranging from 1 (strongly agree) to 6 (strongly disagree); study participants will rate the extent to which they agree or disagree on items. Higher scores indicate more negative appraisals for the career decision-making process. The thirty-five-item CCI scale consists of four factors:

1) Subjective career distress and obstacles (i.e., negative feelings about the pressures or obstacles in decision-making)
2) Active problem-solving (i.e., feelings about a lack of knowledge and information to solve the problem)
3) Academic self-efficacy (i.e., a lack of general academic ability)
4) Career myths (i.e., beliefs about the importance of making a choice and the urgency to decide on careers)

The internal consistency coefficient of CCI was .89 and reliabilities for the four factors ranged from .69 to .90 (Larson et al., 1994). The test-retest reliability of the overall scale was .86, and the stability of the four factors ranged from .68 to .90 (Larson et al., 1994).

Discussion/Summary

In this chapter, the research methodology was discussed. The methodology that was used to obtain the correct data was important. This research methodology helped to address my research questions and hypotheses.

Porter and McKibbin (1988) noted that obtaining a college degree is vitally important to college students and their families; however, there are numerous factors as to why some students complete their degrees and other students do not. The college degree is able to open many doors and avenues for the college graduate.

In addition, employers have long been calling for higher levels of personal and interpersonal skills among the college graduates they hire (Porter and McKibbin, 1988).

The growing importance of world business creates a strong demand for leaders who are sophisticated in international management and skilled at working with people from other countries (Hartog, 2004). The global business environment has changed significantly.

Leading in today's multicultural business environment presents challenges not experienced a generation ago (Gupta, 2009). The comprehensive development of human capital resources is essential to the survival and profitability of the global organization. Organizations need the intellectual and resourcefulness of their human capital. In addition, global organizations need their human capital to perform at a very high level. Many global organizations have human capital in several geographical areas. As such, it is imperative that business leaders understand the importance and dynamics of their human capital.

Boyatzis and Saatcioglu (2008) rejected the notion that effective leaders, managers, and professionals are born that way. In addition, they asserted that through quality competencies training, one could learn to be a better leader, manager, or professional. To test this hypothesis, they built on the earlier longitudinal research studies of Boyatzis, Renio-McKee, and Thompson, 1995, and Boyatzis, Stubbs, and Taylor, 2002. The researchers wanted to show that emotional, social, and cognitive intelligence competencies could be developed in adults. In addition, they identified some "cracks" and a breakdown of the effectiveness shown in earlier studies. These cracks may be attributed to destructive organizational practices.

Peters (2010) studied baby boomers attending colleges. The first-year college students' decision to matriculate and complete a college degree is an important decision. It is one of many important life decisions. There are a number of obstacles that are presented throughout the college students' academic path. There is a convergence of disorientating dilemmas for the college students such as layoffs, business closings, dwindling retirement accounts, declining job market, returning to school, and retirement itself.

These economic factors are increasing the number of older adults looking for retraining at colleges (Peters, 2010). A college education can become the path for this population to be retrained and reengaged in civic and work activities. With a college degree, one is able to attain more financial and personal freedom (Zeiss, 2006). The research methodology that is proposed may help to address whether there is an association between emotional intelligence and the first-year college students' career intentions to complete their degrees.

REFERENCES

Abraham, R. (2000). "The Role of Job Control as a Moderator of Emotional Dissonance and Emotional-Intelligence-Outcome Associations." *Journal of Psychology* 134: 169–184.

Adams, J., H. Khan, R. Raeside, and D. White. (2007). *Research Methods for Graduate Business and Social Science Students* (Los Angeles, CA: SAGE).

Ang, S., and L. Van Dyne. (2008). "Conceptualization of Cultural Intelligence: Definition, Distinctiveness, and Nomological Network." *Handbook of Cultural Intelligence: Theory, Measurement, and Applications*, 3–15.

Arnett, J. (2004). *Emerging Adulthood: The Winding Road from the Late Teens through the Twenties*. New York: Oxford University Press.

Austin, E. (2004). "An Investigation of the Association between Traits of Emotional Intelligence and Emotional Task Performance." *Personality and Individual Differences* 36: 1855–64.

Austin, E., D. Saklofske, S. Huang, and D. McKenney. (2004). "Measurement of Trait of Emotional Intelligence: Testing and Cross-Validating a Modified Version of Schutte et al.'s (1998) Measure." *Personality and Individual Differences* 36: 555–562.

Azniza, I. (2005). "Different Effects of REBT Brief Group Intervention and Behavior Brief Group Intervention toward Maladjustment." Unpublished Doctoral Dissertation, University Science Malaysia.

Banta, T.W. (1993). *Making a Difference: Outcomes of a Decade of Assessment in Higher Education*. San Francisco, CA: Jossey-Bass.

Bar-On, R. (2004). "The Bar-On Emotional Quotient Inventory (EQ-i): Rationale, Description, and Psychometric Properties." In *Measuring Emotional Intelligence: Common Ground and Controversy*, edited by G. Geher.. Hauppauge, NY: Nova Science.

Bastian, V., N. Burns, and T. Nettelbeck. (2005). "Emotional Intelligence Predicts Life Skills, but Not as Well as Personality and Cognitive Abilities." *Personality and Individual Differences* 39: 1135–1145.

Blustein, D. (1989). "The Role of Goal Instability and Career Self-Efficacy in the Career Exploration Process." *Journal of Vocational Behavior* 35: 194–203.

Boyatzis, R.E. (1982). *The Competent Manager: A Model for Effective Performance.* New York, NY: John Wiley & Sons.

Boyatzis, R.E. (2006). "Intentional Change Theory from a Complexity Perspective." *Journal of Management Development* 25: 607–623.

Boyatzis, R.E. (2009). "Competencies as a Behavioral Approach to Emotional Intelligence." *Journal of Management Development* 28: 749–70.

Boyatzis, R.E., A. Renio-McKee, and L. Thompson. (1995). *Past Accomplishments: Establishing the Impact and Baseline of Earlier Programs. Innovation in Professional Education: Steps on a Journey from Teaching to Learning.* San Francisco, CA: Jossey-Bass.

Boyatzis, R., and A. Saatcioglu. (2008). "A 20-Year View of Trying to Develop Emotional, Social and Cognitive Intelligence Competencies in Graduate Management Education." *Journal of Management Development* 27: 92–108.

Boyatzis, R.E., and F. Sala. (2004). "Assessing Emotional Intelligence Competencies." *The Measurement of Emotional Intelligence*: 147–180.

Boyatzis, R.E., E. C. Stubbs, and S. N. Taylor. (2002). "Learning Cognitive and Emotional Intelligence Competencies through Graduate Management Education." *Academy of Management Journal on Learning and Education* 2: 150–162.

Brackett, M., and J. Meyer. (2003). "Convergent, Discriminant, and Incremental Validity of Competing Measures of Emotional Intelligence." *Personality and Social Psychology Bulletin* 29: 1147–58.

Brown, R., and N. Schutte. (2006). "Direct and Indirect Associations between Emotional Intelligence and Subjective Fatigue in University Students." *Journal of Psychosomatic Research* 60: 585–593.

Burns, L. (1994). "Gender Differences among Correlates of Career Indecision." Unpublished doctoral dissertation. Lubbock: Texas Tech University.

Butt, T., and N. Parton. (2005). "Constructivist Social Work and Personal Construct Theory." *British Journal of Social Work* 35: 793–806.

Bye, D., D. Pushkar, and M. Conway. (2007). "Motivation, Interest, and Positive Affect in Traditional and Nontraditional Undergraduate Students." *Adult Education Quarterly* 57: 141–158.

Carmeli, A. (2003). "The Association between Emotional Intelligence and Work Attitudes, Behavior and Outcomes: An Examination among Senior Managers." *Journal of Managerial Psychology* 18: 788–814.

Carmeli, A., and Z. Josman. (2006). "The Association between Emotional Intelligence, Task Performance and Organizational Citizenship Behaviors." *Human Performance* 19: 403–419.

Carnevale, A. (2000). "Community Colleges and Career Qualifications." *New Expeditions: Charting the Second Century of Community Colleges.* Issues Paper No. 11.

Chan, D. (2007). "Leadership Competencies among Chinese Gifted Students in Hong Kong: The Connection with Emotional Intelligence and Successful Intelligence." *Roeper Review* 29 no. 3: 183–189.

Charbonneau, D., and A. Nicol. (2002). "Emotional Intelligence and Prosocial Behaviors in Adolescents." *Psychological Reports* 90: 361–370.

Chartrand, J., S. Robbins, W. Morrill, and K. Boggs. (1990). "Development and Validation of the Career Factors Inventory." *Journal of Counseling Psychology* 37: 491–501.

Chen, C. (1999). "Common Stressors among International College Students: Research and Counseling Implications." *Journal of College Counseling* 2: 49–65.

Chickering, A., and L. Reisser. (1993). *Education and Identity.* 2nd Edition. San Francisco, CA: Jossey-Bass.

Christie, A., P. Jordan, A. Troth, and S. Lawrence. (2007). "Testing the Links between Emotional Intelligence and Motivation." *Journal of Management and Organization* 13: 212–226.

Ciarrochi, J., A. Chan, and J. Bajgar. (2001). "Measuring Emotional Intelligence in Adolescents." *Personality and Individual Differences* 31: 1105–1119.

Ciarrochi, J., A. Chan, and P. Caputi. (2000). "A Critical Evaluation of the Emotional Intelligence Construct." *Personality and Individual Differences* 28: 539–561.

Clark, S., R. Callister, and R. Wallace. (2003). "Undergraduate Management Skills Courses and Students' Emotional Intelligence." *Journal of Management Education* 27: 3–24.

Clyne, C., and N. Blampied. (2004). "Training in Emotion Regulation as a Treatment for Binge Eating: A Preliminary Study." *Behavior Change* 21: 269–281.

Coleman, H. (2010). *Empowering Yourself: The Organizational Game Revealed.* 2nd edition. Bloomington, IN: AuthorHouse.

Colvin, C., and J. Block. (1994). "Do Positive Illusions Foster Mental Health? An Evaluation of Taylor and Brown Formulation. *Psychological Bulletin* 116: 3–20.

Creswell, J. (2008). *Educational Research: Planning, Conducting, and Evaluating Quantitative and Qualitative Research.* 3rd edition. Upper Saddle River, NJ: Pearson Education, Inc.

Daus, C.S., and N. M. Ashkanasy. (2003). "On Deconstructing the Emotional Intelligence 'Debate.'" *Industrial-Organizational Psychologist* 41: 16–18.

Davies, M., L. Stankov, and R. Roberts. (1998). "Emotional Intelligence: In Search of an Elusive Construct." *Personality Processes and Individual Differences* 75 no. 4: 989–1015.

Davis, C., and E. Asliturk. (2011). "Toward a Positive Psychology of Coping with Anticipated Events." *Canadian Psychology* 52: 101–111.

Davis, N., and M. I. Cho. (2005). "Intercultural Competence for Future Leaders of Educational Technology and Its Evaluation." *Interactive Educational Multimedia* 10: 1–22.

Davis, C., and M. Morgan. (2008). "Finding Meaning, Perceiving Growth, and Acceptance of Tinnitus." *Rehabilitation Psychology* 53: 128–138.

Day, A., and S. Carroll. (2004). "Using an Ability-Based Measure of Emotional Intelligence to Predict Individual Performance, Group Performance, and Group Citizenship Behaviors." *Personality and Individual Differences* 41: 1229–39.

Depape, A., J. Hakim-Larson, S. Voelker, S. Page, and D. Jackson. (2006). "Self-Talk and Emotional Intelligence in University Students." *Canadian Journal of Behavioural Science* 38: 250–261.

Dipeolu, A., R. Reardon, I. Sampson, and J. Burkhcad. (2002). "The Association between Dysfunctional Career Thoughts and Adjustment to Disability in College Students with Learning Disabilities." *Journal of Career Assessment* 10: 413–427.

Druskat, V., and J. Wheeler. (2003). "Managing from the Boundary: The Effective Leadership of Self-Managing Work Teams." *Academy of Management Journal* 46: 435–57.

Druskat, V., and S. Wolff. (2001). "Building the Emotional Intelligence of Groups." *Harvard Business Review* 79: 80–90.

Dulewicz, V., and M. Higgs. (2000). "Emotional Intelligence: A Review and Evaluation Study." *Journal of Managerial Psychology* 15 no. 4: 341–372.

Earley, P.C., and S. Ang. (2003). *Cultural Intelligence: Individual Interactions across Cultures.* Palo Alto: Stanford University Press.

Education Trust. (1999). "A Statement of State Education CEO's." *Thinking K–16*: 3, 10.

Elfenbein, H. A., and N. Ambady. (2003). "When Familiarity Breeds Accuracy: Cultural Exposure and Facial Emotion Recognition." *Journal of Personality and Social Psychology* 85: 276–290.

Emmerling, R., and R. Boyatzis. (2012). "Emotional and Social Intelligence Competencies: Cross-Cultural Implications." *Cross Cultural Management* 19: 4–18.

Evelyn, J. (2002). "Nontraditional Students Dominate Undergraduate Enrollments, Study Finds." *Chronicle of Higher Education* 48 no. 3: 246–263.

Fatt, J. (2002). "Emotional Intelligence: For Human Resource Managers." *Management Review News* 25: 57–74.

Faul, F., E. Erdfelder, A. Lang, and A. Buchne. (2007). "G*Power 3: A Flexible Statistical Power Analysis Program for the Social, Behavioral, and Biomedical Sciences." *Behavior Research Methods* 39: 175–191.

Ferdig, R., J. Coutts, J. DiPietro, and B. Lok. (2007). "Innovative Technologies for Multicultural Education Needs." *Multicultural Education & Technology Journal* 1: 47–63.

Forbus, P., J. Newbold, and S. Mehta, S. (2011). "A Study of Non-Traditional and Traditional Students in Terms of Their Time Management Behaviors, Stress Factors, and Coping Strategies." *Academy of Educational Leadership Journal* 15: 109–125.

Fox, F.V., and B. M. Staw. (1979). "The Trapped Administrator: Effects of Job Insecurity and Policy Resistance upon Commitment to a Course of Action." *Administrative Science Quarterly* 24: 449–472.

Gardner, H. (1993). *Multiple Intelligence: The Theory in Practice*. New York, NY: Basic Books.

Gardner, H. (1999). *Intelligence Reframed: Multiple Intelligences for the 21ˢᵗ Century*. New York, NY: Basic Books.

Gati, I., M. Krausz, and S. Osipow. (1996). "A Taxonomy of Difficulties in Career Decision Making." *Journal of Career Psychology* 43: 510–26.

Gelfand, M.J., L. Imai, and R. Fehr. (2008). "Thinking Intelligently about Cultural Intelligence: The Road Ahead," p. 41–55. *Handbook on Cultural Intelligence: Theory, Measurement, and Applications.*

Gianakos, I. (1999). "Patterns of Career Choice and Career Decision-Making Self-Efficacy." *Journal of Vocational Behavior* 54: 244–258.

Goleman, D. (1995). *Emotional Intelligence.* New York, NY: Bantam Books.

Goleman, D. (1998). *What Makes a Leader?* Boston, MA: Harvard Business Review.

Goleman, D. (2000). "Leadership that Gets Results." *Harvard Business Review* 78: 80–90.

Gostick, A., and C. Elton. (2007). *The Carrot Principle.* New York: Free Press.

Grubb, W. (1999). "The Economic Benefits of Subbaccalaureate Education: Results from the National Studies." *Community College Research Center.*

Grubb, W., N. Badway, D. Bell, and M. Castellano. (2000). "Community Colleges Welfare Reform: Emerging Practices, Enduring Problems." *Community College Journal* 69 no. 6: 31–36.

Guastello, D., and S. Guastello. (2003). "Androgyny, Gender Role Behaviour, and Emotional Intelligence among College Students and Their Parents." *Sex Roles* 49: 663–673.

Gupta, S. (2009). *Contemporary Leadership and Intercultural Competence.* Thousand Oaks, CA: SAGE.

Haislett, J., and A. Hafer. (1990). "Predicting Success of Engineering Students during the Freshman Year." *Career Development Quarterly* 39: 86–95.

Hajj, R., and G. Dagher. (2010). "An Empirical Investigation of the Relation between Emotional Intelligence and Job Satisfaction in the Lebanese Service Industry." *The Business Review, Cambridge* 16: 71–78.

Han, K., E. Yang, and S. Choi. (2001). "Research of Attitudes of College Freshmen toward Career Path." *Yonsei University Student Center Research Review* 17: 3–18.

Hannah, L., and L. Robinson. (1990). "Survey Report: How Colleges Help Freshmen Select Courses and Careers." *Journal of Career Planning and Employment* 1: 53–57.

Hartog, D. (2004). "Leading in a Global Context: Vision in Complexity." *Blackwell Handbook of Global Management.*

Hayes, R., J. Nelson, M. Tabin, G. Pearson, and C. Worthy. (2002). "Using School-Wide Data to Advocate for Student Success: Charting the Academic Trajectory of Every Student." *Professional School Counselor* 6 no. 2: 86–94.

Heckhausen, J. (1999). *Developmental Regulation in Adulthood: Age-Normative and Sociostructural Constraints as Adaptive Challenges.* Cambridge, UK: Cambridge University Press.

Heckhausen, J., and R. Schulz. (1995). "A Life-Span Theory of Control." *Psychological Review* 102: 284–304.

Heckhausen, J., and M. Tomasik. (2002). "Get an Apprenticeship before School Is Out: How German Adolescents Adjust Vocational Aspirations When Getting Close to a Development Deadline." *Journal of Vocational Behavior* 60: 199–219.

Hochschild, A. (1983). *The Managed Heart: Commercialization of Human Feelings.* Berkeley, CA: University of California Press.

Holland, J., D. Daiger, and P. Power. (1980). *My Vocational Situation.* Palo Alto, CA: Consulting Psychologists Press.

Janis, I., and L. Mann. (1976). "Coping with Decisional Conflict: An Analysis of How Stress Affects Decision-Making Suggests Interventions to Improve the Process." *American Scientist* 64: 657–666.

Jex, S., and T. Britt. (2008). *Organizational Psychology: A Scientist-Practitioner Approach.* Hoboken, NJ: John Wiley & Sons.

Kilk, K. (1997). "The Association between Dysfunctional Career Thought and Choosing an Academic Major." *Dissertation Abstracts International.*

Kim, E., and K. Oh. (1991). "A Review of Characteristics of the 1991 Yonsei University Entrants." *Yonsei University Counseling Center Research Review* 8: 3–36.

Kirkpatrick, L. (2001). "Multicultural Strategies for Community Colleges: Expanding Faculty Diversity." *ERIC Digest.*

Kolb, D. (1984). *Experiential Learning: Experience as the Source of Learning and Development.* Englewood Cliffs, NJ: Prentice-Hall.

Landy, F.J. (2003). "Emotional Intelligence: A Debate." Paper presented at the 2003 SIOP Conference, Orlando, Florida.

Larsen, J., S. Hemenover, C. Norris, and J. Cacioppo. (2003). "Turning Adversity to Advantage: On the Virtues of the Coactivation of Positive and Negative Emotions." *A Psychology of Human Strengths.* Washington, DC: American Psychological Association.

Larson, L., P. Heppner, T. Ham, and K. Dugan. (1988). "Investigating Multiple Subtypes of Career Indecision through Cluster Analysis." *Journal of Counseling Psychology* 35: 439–446.

Lasonen, J. (2003). "Interculturalisation through Music Teaching." *Lifelong Learning in Europe* 8: 10–16.

Lasonen, J. (2005). "Reflections on Interculturality in Relation to Education and Work." *Higher Education Policy* 18: 397–407.

Law, K., C. Wong, and L. Song. (2004). "The Construct and Criterion Validity of Emotional Intelligence and Its Potential Utility for Management Studies." *Journal of Applied Psychology* 89: 483–496.

Lee, K. (2005). "Coping with Career Indecision: Differences between Four Career Choice Types." *Journal of Career Development* 31: 279–89.

Lee, K., and J. Han. (1997). "Validation of Measurement of Career Attitude Maturity." *Korean Journal of Career Educational Research* 8: 219–255.

Levy-Leboyer, C. (2007). "CQ: Developing Cultural Intelligence at Work." *Personnel Psychology*, 60, 242.

Liau, A.K., A. W. Liau, G. Teoh, and M. T. Liau. (2003). "The Case for Emotional Literacy: The Influence of Emotional Intelligence on

Problem Behaviours in Malaysian Secondary School Students." *Journal of Moral Education* 32: 51–66.

Liff, S. (2003). "Social and Emotional Intelligence: Applications for Developmental Education." *Journal of Developmental Education* 26 no. 3: 28–32.

Likert, R. (1961). *New Patterns of Management.* New York: McGraw-Hill.

Liptak, J. (2005). "Using Emotional Intelligence to Help College Students Succeed in the Workplace." *Journal of Employment Counseling* 42: 171–178.

Locke, D. (1999). *Getting African American Male Students on Track: Working with African-American Males: A Guide to Practice.* Thousand Oaks, CA: SAGE.

Malek, T., I. Noor-Azniza, A. Muntasir, N. Mohammad, and M. Luqman. (2011). "The Effectiveness of Emotional Intelligence Training Program on Social and Academic Adjustment among First Year University Students." *International Journal of Business and Social Science* 2: 251–258.

Manz, C.C., and C. P. Neck. (1991). "Inner Leadership: Creating Productive Thought Patterns." *The Executive* 3: 71.

Markham, S.E., and I. S. Markham. (1995). "Self-Management and Self-Leadership Reexamined. A Level-of-Analysis-Perspective." *Leadership Quarterly* 6: 343–59.

Matthews, G., M. Zeidner, and R. D. Roberts. (2002). *Emotional Intelligence: Science and Myth.* Cambridge, MA: MIT Press.

Mau, W., and D. Jepsen. (1992). "Effects of Computer-Assisted Instruction in Using Formal Decision-Making Strategies to Choose a College Major." *Journal of Counseling Psychology* 39: 185–192.

Mayer, J.D. (1999). "Emotional Intelligence: Popular or Scientific Psychology?" *APA Monitor* 30: 50.

Mayer, J.D., and C. D. Cobb. (2000). "Educational Policy on Emotional Intelligence: Does It Make Sense?" *Educational Psychology Review* 12: 163–183.

Mayer, J., and P. Salovey. (1997). "What Is Emotional Intelligence?" In *Emotional Development and Emotional Intelligence: Implications for Educators*, edited by P. Salovey and D. Sluyter, 3–34. New York, NY: Basic Books.

Mayer, J., P. Salovey, and D. Caruso. (2000). "Competing Models of Emotional Intelligence." *Handbook of Intelligence*, 396–420.

McEnrue, M. P., K. S. Groves, and W. Shen. (2009). "Emotional Intelligence Development: Leveraging Individual Characteristics." *Journal of Management Development* 28: 150–174.

McGregor, D. (1960). "The Human Side of Enterprise." New York: McGraw-Hill.

Mentkowski, M. (2000). *Learning that Lasts: Integrating Learning, Development, and Performance in College and Beyond*. San Francisco, CA: Jossey-Bass.

Meyer, B., and J. Winer. (1993). "The Career Decision Scale and Neuroticism." *Journal of Career Assessment* 1: 171–180.

Momeni, N. (2009). "The Association between Managers' Emotional Intelligence and the Organizational Climate They Create." *Public Personnel Management* 38: 35–48.

Moore, J.W., B. Jensen, and W. Hauck. (1990). "Decision-Making Processes of Youth." *Adolescence* 25: 583–592.

Morris, E., P. Brooks, and J. May. (2003). "The Relationship between Achievement Goal Orientation and Coping Style." *College Student Journal* 37: 3–8.

Neimeyer, R., and S. Baldwin. (2003). "Personal Construct Psychotherapy and the Constructivist Horizon." *International Handbook of Personal Construct Psychology*. Chichester: Wiley.

Nelson, D., and G. Low. (2003). *Emotional Intelligence: Achieving Academic and Career Excellence.* Upper Saddle River, NJ: Prentice Hall.

Newbold, J., S. Mehta, and Forbus. (2010). "A Comparative Study between Non-Traditional Students in Terms of Their Demographics, Attitudes, Behavior and Educational Performance." *International Journal of Education Research* 5 no. 1: 1–24.

Newcombe, M., and N. Ashkanasy. (2002). "The Role of Affect and Affective Congruence in Perceptions of Leaders: An Experimental Study." *Leadership Quarterly* 13: 601–614.

Ng, K., C. Wang, C. Zalaquett, and N. Bodehorn. (2007). "A Confirmatory Factor Analysis of the Wong and Law Emotional Intelligence Scale in a Sample of International College Students." *International Journal for the Advancement of Counseling* 29: 173–185.

Ng, K.Y., and C. P. Earley. (2006). "Culture + Intelligence: Old Constructs, New Frontiers." *Group & Organization Management* 31: 4–19.

Ngunjiri, F., L. Schumacher, and K. Bowman. (2009). "Global Business Leadership: The Need for Emotional and Cultural Intelligence." Paper presented at the International Leadership Association Conference, November 12–15, 2009.

Niederhoffer, K., and J. Pennebaker. (2009). "Sharing One's Story: On the Benefits of Writing or Talking about Emotional Experience." In *Handbook of Positive Psychology,* edited by S. J. Lopez and C.R. Snyder. New York, NY: Oxford University Press.

Oginska-Bulik, N. (2005). "Emotional Intelligence in the Workplace: Exploring Its Effects on Occupational Stress and Health Outcomes in Human Service Workers." *International Journal of Occupational Medicine and Environmental Health* 18: 167–175.

Okpala, C., L. Hopson, and A. Okpala. (2011). "The Impact of Current Economic Crisis on Community Colleges. *College Student Journal* 45: 214–216.

Olson, S. (2009). "Craving for Convenience Fuels Ivy Tech Online Boom." *Indianapolis Business Journal* 29: 18–19.

Osipow, S. (1987). *The Career Decision Scale Manual*. Odessa, FL: Psychological Assessment Resources.

Osipow, S., and J. Winer. (1996). "The Use of the Career Decision Scale in Career Assessment." *Journal of Career Assessment* 4: 117–130.

Paige, R.M. (2004). "The Intercultural in Teaching and Learning: A Developmental Perspective." Paper presented at University of South Australia, Adelaide, 1–15.

Painter, C. (2004). "The Association between Adults Reporting Symptoms of Attention Deficit Hyperactivity Disorder and Dysfunctional Career Beliefs and Job Satisfaction." Dissertation Abstracts International.

Palmer, B., G. Gignac, R. Manocha, and C. Stough. (2005). "A Psychometric Evaluation of the Mayer-Salovey-Caruso Emotional Intelligence Test Version 2.0." *Intelligence* 33: 285–305.

Pascarella, E.T., and P. T. Terenzini. (1991). *How College Affects Students: Findings and Insights from Twenty Years of Research*. San Francisco, CA: Jossey-Bass.

Pau, A., and R. Croucher. (2003). "Emotional Intelligence and Perceived Stress in Dental Undergraduates." *Journal of Dental Education* 67: 1023–1028.

Pedersen, P. (1991). "Counseling International Students." *The Counseling Psychologist* 19: 10–58.

Peters, N. (2010). *Baby Boomers Attending a Community College: Influences, Challenges, and Social Networks*. Doctoral dissertation. Retrieved from ProQuest.

Peterson, G., J. Sampson, J. Lenz, and R. Reardon. (2002). "A Cognitive Information Processing Approach in Career Problem Solving and Decision Making." *Career Choice and Development*. 4th edition. San Francisco, CA: Jossey-Bass.

Phelam, D. (2000). "Enrollment Policy and Student Access at Community Colleges. A Policy Paper." *Education Commission of the States, Center for Community College Policy.*

Polychroniou, P. (2009). "Association between Emotional Intelligence and Transformational Leadership of Supervisors: The Impact on Team Effectiveness." *Team Performance Management* 15: 343–58.

Porter, L., and L. McKibbin. (1988). *Management Education and Development: Drift or Thrust into the 21ˢᵗ Century?* New York, NY: McGraw-Hill.

Poyrazli, S., C. Arbona, R. Bullington, and S. Pisecco. (2001). "Adjustment Issues of Turkish College Students Studying in the United States." *College Student Journal* 35: 52–62.

Quale, A., and A. Schanke. (2010). "Resilience in the Face of Coping with a Severe Physical Injury: A Study of Trajectories of Adjustment in a Rehabilitation Setting." *Rehabilitation Psychology* 55: 12–22.

Reker, G., and P. Wong. (1988). "Aging as an Individual Process: Toward a Theory of Personal Meaning." *Handbook of Theories of Aging.* New York, NY: Springer.

Riley, H., and N. Schutte. (2003). "Low Emotional Intelligence as a Predictor of Substance-Use Problems." *Journal of Drug Education* 33: 391–398.

Roberts, R., M. Zeidner, and G. Matthews. (2001). "Does Emotional Intelligence Meet Traditional Standards for an Intelligence? Some New Data and Conclusions." *Emotions* 1: 196–231.

Saklofske, D., E. Austin, J. Galloway, and K. Davidson. (2007). "Individual Difference Correlates of Health-Related Behaviours: Preliminary Evidence for Links between Emotional Intelligence and Coping." *Personality and Individual Differences* 42: 491–502.

Saklofske, D., E. Austin, and P. Minski. (2003). "Factor Structure and Validity of a Trait Emotional Intelligence Measure." *Personality and Individual Differences* 34: 1091–1100.

Salovey, P., and J. D. Mayer. (1990). "Emotional Intelligence." *Imagination, Cognition, and Personality* 9: 185–211.

Saunders, D., J. Sampson, G. Peterson, and R. Reardon. (2000). "Relation of Depression and Dysfunctional Career Thinking to Career Indecision." *Journal of Vocational Behavior* 56: 288–298.

Schumacher, L., J. Wheeler, and A. Carr. (2009). "The Association between Emotional Intelligence and Buyer's Performance." *Journal of Business & Industrial Marketing* 24: 269–277.

Schutte, N., and J. Malouff. (1998). "Developmental and Interpersonal Aspects of Emotional Intelligence." Presented at the Convention of the American Psychological Society, Washington, DC.

Schutte, N., and J. Malouff. (2002). "Incorporating Emotional Skills in a College Transition Course Enhances Student Retention." *Journal of the First-Year Experience and Students in Transition* 14: 7–21.

Schutte, N., J. Malouff, and N. Bhullar. (2009). "The Assessing Emotions Scale." In *The Assessment of Emotional Intelligence*, edited by C. Stough, D. Sakofske, and J. Parker. New York, NY: Springer Publishing.

Schutte, N., J. Malouff, C. Bobik, T. Conston, C. Greeson, C. Jedlicka, E. Rhodes, and G. Wendorf. (2001). "Emotional Intelligence and Interpersonal Relations." *Journal of Social Psychology* 141: 523–536.

Schutte, N., J. Malouff, L. Hall, D. Haggerty, J. Cooper, C. Golden. (1998). "Development and Validation of a Measure of Emotional Intelligence." *Personality and Individual Differences* 25: 167–177.

Schutte, N., J. Malouff, M. Simunek, J. McKenley, and S. Hollander. (2002). "Characteristic Emotional Intelligence and Emotional Well-Being." *Cognition and Emotion* 16: 769–786.

Scott, G., J. Ciarrochi, and F. Deane. (2004). "Disadvantages of Being an Individualist in an Individualistic Culture: Idiocentrism, Emotional Competence, Stress, and Mental Health." *Australian Psychologist* 39: 143–153.

Seligman, M., and M. Csikzszentmihalyi. (2000). "Positive Psychology: An Introduction." *American Psychologist* 55: 5–14.

Sewell, K. (2003). "An Approach to Posttraumatic Stress." *International Handbook of Personal Construct Psychology*. Chichester: Wiley.

Shipley, N., M. Jackson, and S. Segrest. (2010). "The Effects of Emotional Intelligence, Age, Work Experience, and Academic Performance." *Research in Higher Education Journal* 9: 1–18.

Shivpuri, S., and B. Kim. (2004). "Do Employers and Colleges See Eye-to-Eye? College Student Development and Assessment." *NACE Journal* 65: 37–44.

Sjoberg, L. (2001). "Emotional Intelligence: A Psychometric Analysis." *European Psychologist* 6: 79–95.

Staw, B. (1976). "Knee-Deep in the Big Muddy: The Effect of Personal Responsibility and Decision Consequences upon Commitment to a Previously Chosen Course of Action." *Organizational Behavior and Human Performance* 16: 27–44.

Sternberg, R.J. (2002). Foreword. In *Emotional Intelligence: Science and Myth*, edited by G. Matthews, A. Zeidner, and R. Roberts, xi–xiii. Cambridge, MA: The MIT Press.

Taylor, S., and J. Brown. (1988). "Illusions and Well-Being: A Social Psychological Perspective on Mental Health." *Psychological Bulletin* 103: 193–210.

Thingujam, N., and U. Ram. (2000). "Emotional Intelligence Scale: Indian Norms." *Journal of Education and Psychology* 58: 40–48.

Thorndike, R., and S. Stein. (1937). "An Evaluation of the Attempts to Measure Social Intelligence." *Psychological Bulletin* 34: 275–284.

Totterdell, P., and D. Holman. (2003). "Emotion Regulation in Customer Service Roles: Testing a Model of Emotional Labor." *Journal of Occupational Health Psychology* 8: 55–73.

Tucker, M., J. Sojka, F. Barone, and A. McCarthy. (2000). "Training Tomorrow's Leaders: Enhancing the Emotional Intelligence of Business Graduates." *Journal of Education for Business* 75: 331–37.

US Department of Education, Office of Educational Research and Improvement, National Center for Education Statistics. (1999). "The Condition of Education." http:www.nces.ed.gov/pubs2001/2001022.pdf.

Van Rooy, D., A. Alonso, and C. Viswesvaran. (2005). "Group Differences in Emotional Intelligence Scores: Theoretical and Practical Implications." *Personality and Individual Differences* 38: 689–700.

Vayrynen, R. (1997). *Global Transformation: Economics, Politics, and Culture*. Helsinki: Gaudeamus.

Webb, K. (2009). "Why Emotional Intelligence Should Matter to Management: A Survey of the Literature." *S.A.M. Advanced Management Journal* 74: 32–43.

Wechsler, D. (1943). "Nonintellective Factors in General Intelligence." *Psychological Bulletin* 37: 444–445.

Wechsler, D. (1958). *The Measurement and Appraisal of Adult Intelligence*. 4th edition. Baltimore, MD: The Williams and Wilkins Company.

Williams, J., and M. Luo. (2010). "Understanding First-Year Persistence at a Micropolitan University: Do Geographic Characteristics of Students' Home City Matter?" *College Student Journal* 44: 362–376.

Wing, J., N. Schutte, and B. Byrne. (2006). "The Effect of Positive Writing on Emotional Intelligence and Life Satisfaction." *Journal of Clinical Psychology* 62: 1291–1302.

Winter, D.G., D. C. McClellend, and A. J. Stewart. (1981). *A New Case for the Liberal Arts: Assessing Institutional Goals and Student Development*. San Francisco, CA: Jossey-Bass.

Wong, C.S., and K. S. Law. (2002). "The Effects of Leader and Follower Emotional Intelligence on Performance and Attitude: An Exploratory Study." *Leadership Quarterly* 13: 243–274.

Wrosch, C., and J. Heckhausen. (1999). "Control Processes before and after Passing a Developmental Deadline: Activation and Deactivation of Intimate Association Goals." *Journal of Personality and Social Psychology* 77: 415–427.

Yanchak, K., S. Lease, and D. Strauser. (2005). "Relation of Disability Type and Career Thoughts to Vocational Identity." *Rehabilitation Counseling Bulletin* 48: 130–138.

Yarrish, K., and M. Law. (2009). "An Exploration on the Differences in Emotional Intelligence of First Year Students Examined across Disciplines within the School of Business in a Liberal Arts College." *Contemporary Issues in Education Research* 2: 47–53.

Yurtsever, G. (2003). "Measuring the Moral Entrepreneurial Personality." *Social Behavior and Personality* 31: 1–12.

Yuvaraj, S., and N. Srivastava. (2007). "Are Innovative Managers Emotionally Intelligent?" *Journal of Management Research* 7: 169–178.

Zeiss, T. (2006). "Baby Boomers: An Encore Opportunity." *Community College Journal*: 39–41.

Zizzi, S., H. Deaner, and D. Hirschhorn. (2003). "The Association between Emotional Intelligence and Performance among College Baseball Players." *Journal of Applied Sport Psychology* 15: 262–269.

Printed in the United States
by Baker & Taylor Publisher Services